THE
FOUNDATION
CENTER'S

GUIDE TO
Proposal
Writing

THIRD EDITION

Jane C. Geever

Library of Congress Cataloging-in-Publication Data

Geever, Jane C.
    The Foundation Center's guide to proposal writing—3rd. Ed. / Jane C.
Geever.
        p.   cm.
    Includes bibliographical references.
    ISBN 0-87954-958-0
    1. Proposal writing for grants—United States—Handbooks, manuals,
etc.   I. Title: Guide to proposal writing.   II. Foundation Center.

HG177.5.U6 G44 2001
658.15'224—dc21   2001018978

Contents

Preface

For many years, grantseekers using Foundation Center libraries, our Web site, and print and electronic directories have been asking us for help beyond research into potential funders for their work. They need assistance in writing the proposal and advice on the proper way to submit it, given the widely differing policies and preferences among foundations and corporate grantmakers. To respond to this demand, in 1993 we commissioned Jane C. Geever and Patricia Mc-Neill of the firm, J. C. Geever, Inc., to write a guide for us, based on their many years of fundraising experience and knowledge of a great variety of grantmakers. This third edition includes responses to a new series of interview questions by twice the number of grant-makers and excerpts from a new group of proposals to illustrate the text.

We hope this guide to proposal writing proves useful to all of you who are seeking grants, and we would welcome your comments and reactions to it.

We wish to thank the following grantmakers who participated in the interviews for their time and the valuable insights they provided:

Greg Norton, Grants Administrator
BellSouth Foundation
Atlanta, GA

David Odahowski, President and
    CEO
Edyth Bush Charitable Foundation,
    Inc.
Winter Park, FL

Susan Lajoie Eagan, Executive Vice
    President
The Cleveland Foundation
Cleveland, OH

Rikard Treiber, Deputy Director of
    Grants Management
The Commonwealth Fund
New York, NY

Jessie Bond
(Formerly) Senior Program Officer
The Community Foundation for
    Greater Atlanta
Atlanta, GA

Ruby Lerner, Executive Director
Creative Capital Foundation
New York, NY

J. Andrew Lark, Co-Trustee
The Frances L. & Edwin L.
    Cummings Memorial Fund
New York, NY

Ruth Shack, President
Dade Community Foundation
Miami, FL

Lynn A. Feldhouse, Vice President
    and Secretary
DaimlerChrysler Corporation Fund
Auburn Hills, MI

Kay Dusenbery, Grants/Programs
    Manager
The Danforth Foundation
St. Louis, MO

A. Thomas Hildebrandt, Director
The Davenport-Hatch Foundation,
    Inc.
Rochester, NY

Jonathan T. Howe, Executive
    Director
The Arthur Vining Davis Foundations
Jacksonville, FL

Cynthia Evans, Grants Manager
Geraldine R. Dodge Foundation
Morristown, NJ

David Palenchar, Vice President
El Pomar Foundation
Colorado Springs, CO

John W. Murphy, Executive Director
Flinn Foundation
Phoenix, AZ

Peter F. Bird, Jr., Secretary-Treasurer
The Frist Foundation
Nashville, TN

Reatha Clark King, President and
    Executive Director
General Mills Foundation
Minneapolis, MN

Ilene Mack, Senior Program Officer
William Randolph Hearst Foundation
New York, NY

Elizabeth B. Smith, Executive
   Director
The Hyams Foundation, Inc.
Boston, MA

Hunter W. Corbin, President
The Hyde and Watson Foundation
Chatham, NJ

Heather Graham, Grants Manager
The James Irvine Foundation
San Francisco, CA

Eugene R. Wilson, Senior Vice
   President, Strategic Programs
   and Planning
Ewing Marion Kauffman
   Foundation
Kansas City, MO

Roxanne Ford, Program Director
W. M. Keck Foundation
Los Angeles, CA

Joel J. Orosz, Program Director,
   Philanthropy and Volunteerism
W. K. Kellogg Foundation
Battle Creek, MI

Penelope McPhee, Vice President
   and Chief Program Officer
John S. and James L. Knight
   Foundation
Miami, FL

John E. Marshall III, President
The Kresge Foundation
Troy, MI

Michael Gilligan, Program Director
   for Theology
The Henry Luce Foundation, Inc.
New York, NY

David Ford, President
Lucent Technologies Foundation
Murray Hill, NJ

Elspeth Revere, Director, General
   Program
John D. and Catherine T.
   MacArthur Foundation
Chicago, IL

Julie L. Rogers, President
Eugene and Agnes E. Meyer
   Foundation
Washington, DC

Charles S. Rooks, Executive
   Director
Meyer Memorial Trust
Portland, OR

Hildy Simmons, Managing Director
J.P. Morgan Charitable Trust
New York, NY

Ellen L. Wert, Program Officer
The Pew Charitable Trusts
Philadelphia, PA

Lynn L. Pattillo, President
The Pittulloch Foundation, Inc.
Stone Mountain, GA

Kirke P. Wilson, President and
   Secretary
Rosenberg Foundation
San Francisco, CA

Jane L. Polin, Vice President
S&H greenpoints.com, Inc.
New York, NY

E. Belvin Williams, Executive
   Director
Turrell Fund
Montclair, NJ

Elizabeth C. Reveal, Chief Financial
    Officer and Vice President for
    Management and Evaluation
United Nations Foundation
Washington, DC

Charles H. McTier, President
Robert W. Woodruff Foundation,
    Inc.
Atlanta, GA

We also wish to thank the following nonprofit organizations who graciously permitted us to use excerpts from their proposals to illustrate the text.

Advocates for Children and Youth
Baltimore, MD
Kathryn C. Docie, Director of
    Development

AIDS Resource Foundation for
    Children
Newark, NJ
Terrence P. Zealand, Executive
    Director

Alternatives for Community &
    Environment, Inc.
Roxbury, MA
Penn Loh, Executive Director

Ballet of the Dolls
Minneapolis, MN
Craig Harris, Executive Director

Center for Responsive Politics
Washington, DC
Ellen S. Miller, Executive Director

The Children's Institute
Verona, NJ
Dr. Bruce Ettinger, Executive
    Director

Claremont Neighborhood Centers,
    Inc.
Bronx, NY
Rachel E. Spivey, Executive
    Director

Community Bridges
Silver Spring, MD
Naomi Nim, Executive Director

Community IMPACT!
Washington, DC
Greg Taylor, Executive Director

The Community Projects
    Foundation, Inc.
Columbus, GA
Thomas B. Black, Executive
    Director

DC Heritage Tourism Coalition
Washington, DC
Kathryn S. Smith, Executive
    Director

Detroit Zoological Society
Royal Oak, MI
Jane Alessandrini, Director of
    Development

District of Columbia Arts Center
Washington, DC
B. Stanley, Executive Director

The Field
New York, NY
Katherine Longstreth, Director of
    Art-Based Programs

Heads Up
Washington, DC
Vincent Pan, Executive Director

Hualapai Tribal Health Department
Peach Springs, AZ
Sandra Yellowhawk, Director

Jobs for Youth-Boston, Inc.
Boston, MA
Gary Kaplan, Executive Director
Paula Paris, Director of
Development

Long Island Fund for Women &
Girls
Bethpage, NY
Diane Cohen, Executive Director

Louisville Seminary
Louisville, KY
Dianne Reistroffer, Dean of the
Seminary

Madison School District #38
Phoenix, AZ
Kay Coleman, Assistant
Superintendent for Educational
Services

The Minnesota Opera
Minneapolis, MN
Kevin Smith, President and CEO

Morristown Neighborhood House
Morristown, NJ
Christopher D. Mobley, Director of
Development

Multicultural Youth Tour of What's
Now (MYTOWN)
Boston, MA
Karilyn Crockett, Director

Museum of Science
Boston, MA
Ben Brooks, Senior Grants
Associate

New York Botanical Garden
Bronx, NY
Gregory Long, President

Operation Exodus Inner City, Inc.
New York, NY
Luis Iza, Jr., Executive Director

Project Renewal
New York, NY
Edward I. Geffner, Executive
Director

Ronald McDonald House of New
York
New York, NY
Vivian Harris, Executive Director

San Francisco Theological
Seminary
San Anselmo, CA
James G. Emerson, Jr., President
(Interim)

WomenVenture
St. Paul, MN
Tené Heidelberg, President

YWCA of Plainfield/North
Plainfield
Plainfield, NJ
Jacquelyn M. Glock, Executive
Director

From the Author

Proposal writing is essential to the fundraising process, but it can be intimidating for the novice. There is nothing worse than staring at a blank piece of paper or computer screen with the sinking feeling that so much is riding on the prose you must create. Yet, if you follow the step-by-step process described in this book, you can create a proposal with a minimum of anxiety.

Take the steps one at a time. You will be successful in writing exciting and compelling proposals, proposals that will capture the interest of foundations and corporations, proposals that will generate grant support for your nonprofit organization.

In preparing this book, I interviewed a cross section of foundation and corporate representatives to find out their current thoughts on what should go into a proposal. While this material reinforces the steps I describe for writing a proposal, it also presents some notable insights into how grantmakers do their work, the challenges facing funders today, and how they are responding. These insights are a distinguishing feature of this book: they show the reality of the fundraising process from the funder's side of the proposal.

The 39 funding representatives interviewed include a geographic mix of local and national foundations, three community foundations, and six corporate givers. Some of the funders represented have been in existence for many years. Others are fairly new. All are large enough to have at least one person on staff, and some employ many people.

While the grantmakers interviewed reflect a relatively broad spectrum, it is important to remember that there are more than 53,000 private foundations in the United States. The majority of these have no staff and in fact are so small that the few local grants they award each year can be handled by trustees, lawyers, or family members. Therefore, the comments made here do not necessarily apply to all funders, but they do provide an indication of how some of the larger funders operate and how they evaluate the proposals they receive.

A series of questions was designed for the interview sessions in order to elicit views not only on proposal writing but also on the entire funding process and particularly on the impact of new technologies on this process. Interviews were conducted via the telephone, following a questionnaire format. Questions were posed as to desired proposal contents, layout, length, and presentation. Funders were asked how proposals captured and kept their attention, what the characteristics of a successful proposal are, and what red flags are raised when they read proposals. They were also asked to discuss follow-up strategies once an agency receives a grant and whether, and how, to resubmit a rejected proposal. They were asked to describe trends they perceived in the funding climate for the millennium.

Information and quotes gleaned from these interviews are used throughout the text. Chapter 13, "What the Funders Have to Say," reflects the substance of the interviews. Here, the reader will find specific questions asked of each grantmaking representative with some of their responses. The goal in presenting this information is distinctly not to help the reader learn about particular funders but rather to provide a more general sense of grantmakers' perspectives on proposal writing. The funders interviewed have spoken frankly.

They have all granted permission to the Foundation Center to use their quotes.

Acknowledgments

I would like to express appreciation to the staff of J. C. Geever, Inc., particularly to Cheryl Austin who helped prepare the manuscript, and to Judi Margolin, Margaret Morth, and Cheryl Loe of the Foundation Center who saw this guide through production.

Introduction

If you are reading this book, you probably have already decided that foundations should be part of your fundraising strategy. You should be aware that, together, foundations and corporations provide only about 16.2 percent of private gift support to nonprofit institutions. Their support, however, can be extremely important in augmenting other forms of income, in permitting major new initiatives, or simply in promoting the mission of your agency.

Foundation giving has increased dramatically in recent years. During the decade of the 1990s, more than 5,400 foundations with assets over $1 million or annual grants budgets of $100,000 or more were created. The assets of the foundation field nearly tripled between 1990 and 1998 both because of these new players and because of the rise in the value of the assets held by existing foundations. By 1998, foundations held combined assets of over $385 billion. For 1999, their estimated giving totaled approximately $23 billion.

Unfortunately, competition for these grant dollars has also increased. Many nonprofits are being created to deal with new or heightened social needs. Cutbacks in government funding for nonprofit services and activities have meant that many groups that previously relied primarily on government funds are now turning to private sources to support their work.

In comparison with the figures for foundation giving, according to the American Association of Fund-Raising Counsel (AAFRC) Trust for Philanthropy, giving by individuals was $159.3 billion in 1999, eight times that of foundations. There is lots of money out there. What you need to attract it to your agency is a comprehensive fundraising strategy that includes a variety of sources and approaches. This book focuses on how to create proposals to win foundation and corporate support.

You will want to tell your story clearly, keeping the interests of those you are approaching in mind. You need to recognize the potential for partnership with those you are approaching.

The Proposal Is Part of a Process

The subject of this book is proposal writing. But the proposal does not stand alone. It must be part of a process of planning and of research on, outreach to, and cultivation of, potential foundation and corporate donors.

This process is grounded in the conviction that a partnership should develop between the nonprofit and the donor. When you spend a great deal of your time seeking money, it is hard to remember that it can also be difficult to give money away. In fact, the dollars contributed by a foundation or corporation have no value until they are attached to solid programs in the nonprofit sector.

This truly *is* an ideal partnership. The nonprofits have the ideas and the capacity to solve problems, but no dollars with which to implement them. The foundations and corporations may have the financial resources but not necessarily the other resources needed to create programs. Bring the two together effectively, and the result is a dynamic collaboration. Frequently, the donor is transformed into a stakeholder in the grantee organization, becoming deeply interested and involved in what transpires.

"We think of nonprofits as our partners," says Cynthia Evans of the Geraldine R. Dodge Foundation. "Once we have given a grant, there is a lot more we can do for our grantees." Salin Geevarghese, formerly of BellSouth Foundation and now with the Conservation Company, has this advice: "Manage the relationship with the grant-maker. It is worth the effort to be strategic. Identify those potential donors who will be interested for the long term."

Other funders speak of investing in people. In the opinion of Julie Rogers of the Eugene and Agnes E. Meyer Foundation, "Giving is one human to another." And Reatha Clark King of the General Mills Foundation draws attention to the interconnection among the ideas of relationship, partnership, and trust. She refers to these concepts as "heavy-duty words."

You need to follow a step-by-step process in the search for private dollars. It takes time and persistence to succeed. After you have written a proposal, it could take a year or more to obtain the funds needed to carry it out. And even a perfectly written proposal submitted to the right prospect might be rejected for any number of reasons.

Raising funds is an investment in the future. Your aim should be to build a network of foundation and corporate funders, many of which give small gifts on a fairly steady basis, and a few of which give large, periodic grants. By doggedly pursuing the various steps of the process, each year you can retain most of your regular supporters and strike a balance with the comings and goings of larger donors. The distinctions between support for basic, ongoing operations and special projects are discussed elsewhere in this book. For now, keep in mind that corporate givers and small family foundations tend to be better prospects for annual support than the larger, national foundations.

The recommended process is not a formula to be rigidly adhered to. It is a suggested approach that can be adapted to fit the needs of any nonprofit and the peculiarities of each situation. Fundraising is an art, not a science. You must bring your own creativity to it and remain flexible.

An example might help. It is recommended that you attempt to speak with the potential funder prior to submitting your proposal. The purpose of your call is to test your hypothesis gleaned from your research about the potential match between your nonprofit organization and the funder. Board member assistance, if you are fortunate enough to have such contacts, ordinarily would not come into play until a much later stage. But what do you do if a board member indicates that his law partner is chairman of the board of a foundation you plan to approach? He offers to submit the proposal directly to his partner. You could refuse the offer and plod through the next steps, or you could be flexible in this instance, recognizing that your agency's likelihood of being funded by this foundation might have just risen dramatically. Don't be afraid to take the risk.

Recognizing the importance of the process to the success of your agency's quest for funds, let's take a look at each step.

Step One: Setting Funding Priorities

In the planning phase, you need to map out all of your agency's priorities, whether or not you will seek foundation or corporate grants for them. Ideally these priorities are determined in an annual planning session. The result of the meeting should be a solid consensus on the funding priorities of your organization for the coming year. Before seeking significant private sector support, you need to decide which of your organization's funding priorities will translate into good proposals. These plans or projects are then developed into funding proposals, and they form the basis of your foundation and corporate donor research.

Step Two: Drafting the Basic or "Master" Proposal

You should have at least a rough draft of your proposal in hand before you proceed, so that you can be really clear about what you'll be asking funders to support. In order to develop a "master" proposal, you will need to assemble detailed background information on the project, select the proposal writer, and write the actual components of the document, including the executive summary, statement of need, project description, budget, and organizational information.

Step Three: Packaging the Proposal

At this juncture you have laid the groundwork for your application. You have selected the projects that will further the goals of your organization. You have written the master proposal, usually a "special project" proposal, or a variation, such as one for a capital campaign or endowment fund.

Before you can actually put the document together and get it ready to go out the door, you will need to tailor your "master" proposal to the specific funder's priorities. When you have taken that step, you will need to add a cover letter and, where appropriate, an appendix, paying careful attention to the components of the package and how they are put together.

Step Four: Researching Potential Funders

You are now ready to identify those sources that are most likely to support your proposal. You will use various criteria for developing your list, including the funders' geographic focus and their demonstrated interest in the type of project for which you are seeking funds. This research process will enable you to prepare different finished proposal packages based on the guidelines of specific funders.

Step Five: Contacting and Cultivating Potential Funders

This step saves you unnecessary or untimely submissions. Taking the time to speak with a funder about your organization and your planned proposal submission sets the tone for a potentially supportive future relationship, *if* they show even a glimmer of interest in your project. This step includes judicious use of phone and/or e-mail communication, face-to-face meetings, board contacts, and written updates and progress reports. Each form of cultivation is extremely important and has its own place in the fundraising process. Your goal in undertaking this cultivation is to build a relationship with the potential donor. Persistent cultivation keeps your agency's name in front of the foundation or corporation. By helping the funder learn more about your group and its programs, you make it easier for them to come to a positive response on your proposal—or, failing that, to work with you in the future.

Step Six: Responding to the Result

No matter what the decision from the foundation or corporate donor, you must assume responsibility for taking the next step. If the response is positive, good follow-up is critical to turning a mere grant into a true partnership.

Unfortunately, even after you have followed all of the steps in the process, statistically the odds are that you will learn via the mail or a phone call that your request was denied. Follow-up is important here, too, either to find out if you might try again at another time or with another proposal or to learn how to improve your chances of getting your proposal funded by others.

1

Getting Started: Establishing a Presence and Setting Funding Priorities

Every nonprofit organization needs to raise money. That is a given. Yet some nonprofits believe that their group must look special or be doing something unique before they are in a position to approach foundations and corporate grantmakers for financial support. This assumption is mistaken. If your organization is meeting a valid need, you are more than likely ready to seek foundation or corporate support.

But three elements should already be in place. First, your agency should have a written mission statement. Second, your organization should have completed the process of officially acquiring nonprofit status, or you need to have identified an appropriate fiscal agent to receive the funds on your behalf. Finally, you should have credible program or service achievements or plans in support of your mission.

Mission Statement

When your agency was created, the founders had a vision of what the organization would accomplish. The mission statement is the written summary of that vision. It is the global statement from which all of your nonprofit's programs and services flow. Such a statement enables you to convey the excitement of the purpose of your nonprofit, especially to a potential funder who has not previously heard of your work. Of course, for you to procure a grant, the foundation or corporation must agree that the needs being addressed are important ones.

Acquiring Nonprofit Status

The agency should be incorporated in the state in which you do business. In most states this means that you create bylaws and have a board of directors. It is easy to create a board by asking your close friends and family members to serve. A more effective board, though, will consist of individuals who care about the cause and are willing to work to help your organization achieve its goals. They will attend board meetings, using their best decision-making skills to build for success. They will actively serve on committees. They will support your agency financially and help to raise funds on its behalf. Potential funders will look for this kind of board involvement.

In the process of establishing your nonprofit agency, you will need to obtain a designation from the federal Internal Revenue Service that allows your organization to receive tax-deductible gifts. This designation is known as 501(c)(3) status. A lawyer normally handles this filing for you. Legal counsel can be expensive. However, some lawyers are willing to provide free help or assistance at minimal cost to organizations seeking 501(c)(3) status from the IRS.

Once your nonprofit has gone through the filing process, you can accept tax-deductible gifts. If you do not have 501(c)(3) status and are not planning to file for it in the near future, you can still raise funds. You will need to find another nonprofit with the appropriate IRS designation willing to act as a fiscal agent for grants received by your agency. How does this work? Primary contact will be between your organization and the funder. The second agency, however, agrees to be responsible for handling the funds and providing financial reports. The funder will require a formal written statement from the agency serving as fiscal agent. Usually the fiscal agent will charge your organization a fee for this service.

Credible Programs

Potential funders will want to know about programs already in operation. They will invest in your agency's future based on your past achievements. You will use the proposal to inform the funder of your accomplishments, which should also be demonstrable if an on-site visit occurs.

If your organization is brand new or the idea you are proposing is unproven, the course you plan to take must be clear and unambiguous. Your plan must be achievable and compelling. The expertise of those involved must be relevant. Factors such as these must take the place of a track record when one does not yet exist. Funders are often willing to take a risk on a new idea, but be certain that you can document the importance of the idea and the strength of the plan.

Like people, foundations have different levels of tolerance for risk. Some will invest in an unknown organization because the proposed project looks particularly innovative. Most, however, want assurance that their money is going to an agency with strong leaders who have proven themselves capable of implementing the project described in the proposal.

What really makes the difference to the potential funder is that your nonprofit organization has a sense of direction and is implementing, or has concrete plans to implement, programs that matter in our society. You have to be able to visualize exciting programs and to articulate them via your proposal. Once you've got these three elements in place, you're ready to raise money from foundations and corporations!

Setting Funding Priorities

Once your organization has established a presence, the first step of the proposal process is determining the priorities of your organization. Only after you do that can you select the right project or goals to turn into a proposal.

3

Your Priorities

There is one rule in this process: You must start with your organization's needs and then seek funders that will want to help with them. Don't start with a foundation's priorities and try to craft a project to fit them. Chasing the grant dollar makes little sense from the perspectives of fundraising, program design, or agency development.

When you develop a program tailored to suit a donor, you end up with a project that is critically flawed. First, in all likelihood the project will be funded only partially by the grant you receive. Your organization is faced with the dilemma of how to fund the rest of it. Further, it will likely be hard to manage the project as part of your total program without distorting your other activities. Scarce staff time and scarcer operating funds might have to be diverted from the priorities you have already established. At worst, the project might conflict with your mission statement.

Start with a Planning Session

A planning session is an excellent way to identify the priorities for which you will seek foundation grants and to obtain agencywide consensus on them. Key board members, volunteers, and critical staff, if your agency has staff, should come together for a several-hour discussion. Such a meeting will normally occur when the budget for the coming fiscal year is being developed. In any case, it cannot be undertaken until the overall plan and priorities for your organization are established.

The agenda for the planning session is simple. With your organization's needs and program directions clearly established, determine which programs, needs, or activities can be developed in proposal form for submission to potential funders.

Apply Fundability Criteria

Before moving ahead with the design of project proposals, test them against a few key criteria:

1. The money cannot be needed too quickly. It takes time for funders to make a decision about awarding a grant. If the foundation or corporate grantmaker does not

know your agency, a cultivation period will probably
be necessary.

A new program can take several years to be fully
funded, unless specific donors have already shown an
interest in it. If your new program needs to begin
immediately, foundation and corporate donors might
not be logical sources to pursue. You should begin
with other funding, from individuals, churches, or
civic groups, from earned income, or from your own
operating budget, or else you should delay the start-up
until funding is secured from a foundation or
corporate grantmaker.

A project that is already in operation and has
received foundation and corporate support stands a
better chance of attracting additional funders within a
few months of application. Your track record will
provide a new funder with an easy way to determine
that your nonprofit can deliver results.

2. Specific projects tend to be of greater interest to most
   foundation and corporate funders than are general
   operating requests. This fundraising fact of life can be
   very frustrating for nonprofits that need dollars to
   keep their doors open and their basic programs and
   services intact. There is no doubt, though, that it is
   easier for the foundation or corporate funder to make a
   grant when the trustees will be able to see precisely
   where the money is going, and the success of their
   investment can be more readily assessed.

   Keep in mind the concerns of the foundation and
   corporate funders about this question when you are
   considering how to develop your proposals for them.
   You may have to interpret the work of your
   organization according to its specific functions. For
   example, one nonprofit agency uses volunteers to
   advocate in the courts on behalf of children in the
   foster care system. Its goal is to bring about permanent
   solutions to the children's situations. When this
   agency first secured grants from foundations and
   corporations, it did so for general support of its
   program. Finding supporters reluctant to continue

5

providing general support once the program was launched, the staff began to write proposals for specific aspects of the agency's work, such as volunteer recruitment, volunteer training, and advocacy, thus making it easier for donors to continue to fund ongoing, core activities.

Some foundations do give general operating support. You will use the print and electronic directories, Web sites, annual reports, the foundations' own 990-PFs, and other resources described elsewhere in this book to target those that are true candidates for operating and annual support requests, if you find that your funding priorities cannot be packaged into projects. Alternatively, your general operating dollars *might* have to come from nonfoundation sources.

3. Support from individual donors and government agencies might be better sources for some of the priorities you are seeking to fund. Moreover, having a diverse base of funding support is beneficial to the financial well-being of your nonprofit agency. Foundation and corporation support usually will not take the place of support from individuals in the form of personal gifts raised via face-to-face solicitation, special events, and direct mail and/or by earned income in the form of fees or dues.

You know the priorities of your organization. You have determined which ones should be developed for submission to foundations and corporations in the form of a proposal. You are now ready to move on to the proposal-writing step.

2

Developing the Master Proposal: Preparation, Tips on Writing, Overview of Components

One advantage of preparing the master proposal before you approach any funders is that all of the details will have been worked out. You will have the answers to just about any question posed to you about this project.

Another advantage is that usually you will need to customize only the cover letter, to reflect the connection between your agency and that particular funder or to take note of its specific program priorities. Few funders require a separate application form or special format.

Gathering Background Information

The first thing you will need to do in writing the master proposal is to gather the documentation for it. You will require background documentation in three areas: concept, program, and expenses.

If all of this information is not readily available to you, determine who will help you gather each type of information. If you are part of a small nonprofit with no staff, a knowledgeable board member will be the logical choice. If you are in a larger agency, there should be program and financial support staff who can help you. Once you know with whom to talk, identify the questions to ask.

This data-gathering process makes the actual writing much easier. And by involving other stakeholders in the process, it also helps key people within your agency seriously consider the project's value to the organization.

Concept

It is important that you have a good sense of how the project fits into the philosophy and mission of your agency. The need that the proposal is addressing must also be documented. These concepts must be well-articulated in the proposal. Funders want to know that a project reinforces the overall direction of an organization, and they might need to be convinced that the case for the project is compelling. You should collect background data on your organization and on the need to be addressed so that your arguments are well-documented.

Program

Here is a checklist of the program information you require:

- the nature of the project and how it will be conducted;
- the timetable for the project;
- the anticipated outcomes and how best to evaluate the results; and
- staffing and volunteer needs, including deployment of existing staff and new hires.

Expenses

You will not be able to pin down all of the expenses associated with the project until the program details and timing have been worked out. Thus, the main financial data gathering takes place after the narrative part of the master proposal has been written. However, at this stage you do need to sketch out the broad outlines of the budget to be sure that the costs are in reasonable proportion to the outcomes you anticipate. If it appears that the costs will be prohibitive, even anticipating a foundation grant, you should then scale back your plans or adjust them to remove the least cost-effective expenditures.

Deciding Who Will Write the Proposal

While gathering data, you can make the decision about who will actually write the document. You might decide to ask someone else to draft it for you. This is a tough decision. If the obvious staff member you identify to write the first draft will have to put aside some other major task, it might not be cost-effective for the agency, and you might consider whether someone else on staff is a skilled writer or a willing learner and could be freed up from routine assignments.

If you lack a staff member with the skills and time to take on the task, a volunteer or board member might be an excellent alternative. You will need to identify someone who knows the agency and writes well. You will spend substantial time with this person, helping to describe the kind of document you want. In the long run, this can be time well spent, because you now have identified a willing and skilled volunteer proposal writer.

If you have found your writer on staff or among your volunteer ranks, you are all set. The information for the proposal has been gathered, and work can commence. Should you fail to find someone this way, then an outsider will be needed. Bear in mind, before you choose this option, that the most successful proposals are often "home grown," even if they aren't perfect. A too-slick proposal obviously written by an outsider can be a real turnoff to funders.

On the other hand, while someone inside your agency will always know your organization better than a consultant, an outsider can bring objectivity to the process and may write more easily, especially with the data gathering already complete. Once the decision is made to use a consultant, you will need to make a list of prospective consultants, interview the leading candidates, check references, and make your selection.

You and the consultant will develop a contract that adequately reflects the proposed relationship. This document should include:

- details on the tasks to be performed by the consultant;
- the date when the contract becomes effective and the date of its expiration;
- a cancellation clause that can be exercised by either party within a specific number of days' notice, usually not less than 30 or more than 90 days;
- a statement that the agency owns the resulting proposal;
- information on the fee that the consultant will be paid and when it is to be paid (perhaps tying it to delivery of the product or completion of specified tasks);
- details on reimbursement of out-of-pocket expenses or on an expense advance on which the consultant may draw; and
- a provision for the contract to be signed both by the consultant and by an officer of the nonprofit.

If possible, your nonprofit organization should use legal counsel in developing the contract. At a minimum, an attorney should review the document to see that the agency's interests are protected. Seek out *pro bono* legal assistance, if need be. Do not consider oral agreements to be binding on either side. Put everything in writing.

Tips on Writing the Proposal

Regardless of who writes the proposal, grant requests are unique documents. They are unlike any other kind of writing assignment. Here are some tips for the proposal writer:

For many grantseekers, the proposal is the *only* opportunity to communicate with a foundation or corporate donor.

The written document is the one thing that remains with a funder after all the meetings and telephone calls have taken place. It must be self-explanatory. It must reflect the agency's overall image. Your proposal will educate the funder about your project and agency. It should motivate the potential funder to make a gift.

You do need to put as much care into preparing your proposal as you have put into designing the project and as you are planning to put into operating it. You have spent a fair amount of time determining priorities for raising funds and gathering the appropriate information for the proposal. The information you have collected should be thoroughly woven into an integrated whole that dramatically depicts your agency's project for the funder.

There are some basic rules that apply to all writing and a few that are unique to proposals for foundations and corporations.

Get Your Thoughts Sorted Out

A proposal must deliver critical ideas quickly and easily. Your writing must be clear if you want others to understand your project and become excited by it. It will be hard to accomplish this if you have not clarified your thoughts in advance.

This means identifying the central point of your proposal. All of your subsequent points should flow easily from it. Once you have clearly thought through the broad concepts of the proposal, you are ready to prepare an outline.

Outline What You Want to Say

You understand the need for the program. You have already gathered the facts about how it will unfold, if funded. You have identified the benchmarks of success and the financial requirements. With this information in hand, outline what should be said and in what order. If you take the time to create this outline, the process of writing will be much easier, and the resulting proposal will be stronger. Rushing to write a document without an outline only leads to frustration, confusion, and a poorly articulated proposal.

Avoid Jargon

Jargon confuses the reader and hampers his or her ability to comprehend your meaning. It impedes your style. It may be viewed as pretentious. With so much at stake in writing a proposal, it makes sense to avoid words (and acronyms) that are not generally known and to select words for their precision.

Be Compelling, but Don't Overstate Your Case

People give to people. While your proposal has to present the facts, it must let the human element shine through. Personify the issue. Tell your story with examples. Illuminate your vision so that the funder can share it with you. Don't be afraid to humanize the materials once the facts are in place. But never assume that your writing is so compelling that programmatic details are unnecessary. A number of the grantmakers interviewed for this guide indicated a preference for real-life examples to enhance the text of a proposal. In the words of Julie Rogers of the Eugene and Agnes E. Meyer Foundation, "The human dimension should come through. A compelling story sticks out."

Try to be realistic in presenting your case. Take care that in your enthusiasm you do not overstate the need, the projected outcomes, or the basic facts about your organization.

It is dangerous to promise more than you can deliver. The proposal reviewer is sure to raise questions, and the result could be damaged credibility with the funder. Worse, if the proposal is funded, and the results do not live up to the exaggerated expectations, future support is jeopardized.

Keep It Simple

In the old days, fundraisers believed that the longer the document and the more detail it had, the better it was and the more money could be requested. Today, foundation and corporate funders look for concisely presented ideas. Eliminate wordiness. Simply present the key thoughts.

Keep It Generic

As you progress through the fundraising process, you may well approach a number of different potential funders with the same or a similar proposal. Thus, it makes sense to develop a master proposal that, with certain customizing touches, can be submitted to a number of sources. Some funders today are even beginning to accept master proposals submitted online.

In some areas of the country, groups of foundations have agreed to adopt a common application form. It makes sense to inquire as to whether one exists in your geographic area and whether the funder you are applying to accepts proposals in this form. The very same careful research that goes into identifying appropriate funders pertains to contacting those that accept common application forms. Examples of common application forms can be found at the Foundation Center's World Wide Web site at http://www.fdncenter.org.

COMPONENTS OF A PROPOSAL

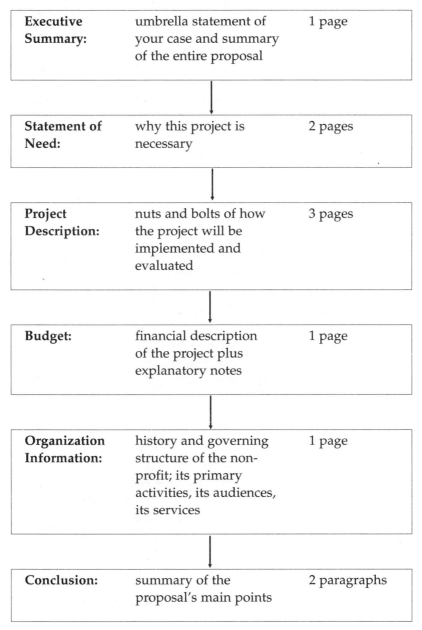

Executive Summary:	umbrella statement of your case and summary of the entire proposal	1 page

Statement of Need:	why this project is necessary	2 pages

Project Description:	nuts and bolts of how the project will be implemented and evaluated	3 pages

Budget:	financial description of the project plus explanatory notes	1 page

Organization Information:	history and governing structure of the non-profit; its primary activities, its audiences, its services	1 page

Conclusion:	summary of the proposal's main points	2 paragraphs

Revise and Edit

Once you have completed the proposal, put it away temporarily. Then in a day or two, reread it with detachment and objectivity, if possible. Look for the logic of your arguments. Are there any holes? Move on to analyzing word choices and examining the grammar. Finally, give the document to someone else to read. Select someone with well-honed communication skills, who can point out areas that remain unclear and raise unanswered questions. Ask for a critical review of the case and of the narrative flow. This last step will be most helpful in closing any gaps, in eliminating jargon, and in heightening the overall impact of the document.

A well-crafted document should result from all these hours of gathering, thinking and sifting, and writing and rewriting. Carol Robinson, former executive director of the Isaac H. Tuttle Fund, provided us with an ideal to strive for that is still very telling today: "To me a proposal is a story. You speak to the reader and tell the reader a story, something you want him/her to visualize, hear, feel. It should have dimension, shape and rhythm and, yes, it should 'sing.'" (private letter, December 30, 1985)

The following chapters include many examples to assist you in better understanding the points being made. A number of these are excerpts from actual proposals and are reprinted with permission from the issuing agency. Please note that to keep the design of the book simple, we did not reproduce these examples in their original formats.

No two proposals are precisely the same in their execution, and no single proposal is absolutely perfect. In fact, some of the examples presented here have flaws. These examples are used to underscore a specific point, but together they illustrate the more general one that flexibility on the part of the proposal writer is essential. In a winning proposal, often the nature of the issues being addressed overrides rules about format.

A full sample proposal appears in Appendix A.

3

Developing the Master Proposal: The Executive Summary

This first page of the proposal is the most important section of the entire document. Here you will provide the reader with a snapshot of what is to follow. Specifically, it summarizes all of the key information and is a sales document designed to convince the reader that this project should be considered for support. Be certain to include:

Problem—a brief statement of the problem or need your agency has recognized and is prepared to address (one or two paragraphs);

Solution—a short description of the project, including what will take place and how many people will benefit from the program, how and where it will operate, for how long, and who will staff it (one or two paragraphs);

Funding requirements—an explanation of the amount of grant money required for the project and what your plans are for funding it in the future (one paragraph); and

Organization and its expertise—a brief statement of the name, history, purpose, and activities of your agency and its capacity to carry out this proposal (one paragraph).

How will the executive summary be used? First, in the initial review of your request, it will enable the funder to determine that the proposal is within its guidelines. Then it is often forwarded to other staff or board members to assist in their general review of the request. If you don't provide a summary, someone at the funder's office may well do it for you and emphasize the wrong points.

Here's a tip: It is easier to write the executive summary last. You will have your arguments and key points well in mind. It should be concise. Ideally, the summary should be no longer than one page or 300 words.

Here is an example of an executive summary, taken from a proposal submitted by Project Renewal to the Frances L. & Edwin L. Cummings Memorial Fund. This summary immediately identifies the financial request. It provides an excellent synopsis of the problem and the proposed solution.

Project Renewal

Proposal: MedVan Social Worker

Project Renewal requests from the Francis L. & Edwin L. Cummings Memorial Fund a grant of $25,000 to support the addition of a Social Worker to our Mobile Medical Outreach Clinic—or *MedVan,* as it is known on the streets of New York.

Launched in 1986, MedVan was the nation's first mobile medical clinic to serve homeless people, providing primary care and referrals to thousands of indigent New Yorkers on the street, and in the shelters, soup kitchens, and drop-in centers where they congregate.

Two critical factors make it urgently necessary to break more new ground by adding a Social Worker to MedVan's professional team: first, MedVan's patients are displaying ever more complex suites of medical problems, often requiring multiple

---

visits and long term care to arrive at a complete diagnosis and treatment—a situation that has severely stretched the capacity of MedVan's medical professionals; second, though MedVan patients often qualify for medical entitlements and other public services, they frequently need help in obtaining them—a need that MedVan's medical team has valiantly tried to satisfy, while also trying to meet an ever more demanding patient load.

Adding a Social Worker to MedVan will solve these problems by:

- Helping significantly more patients to obtain entitlements and other services;

- Tracking patients through referrals, which will encourage them to take full advantage of available services;

- Freeing the MedVan team to treat more patients;

- Resulting in more repeat patients, which will enable the MedVan team to perform more complete diagnoses and treatment.

The ultimate benefit of this initiative will be improved health among MedVan's homeless patients. This is an absolutely essential step in the process of helping homeless people to rehabilitate themselves—which is Project Renewal's mission.

Another example comes from a proposal written for the Eugene and Agnes E. Meyer Foundation by Community Bridges.

Proposal Summary

Community Bridges plans to continue and expand *Jump Start Girls! Adelante Ninas!* In the 1999–2000 school year sixty girls in grades 4–7 will attend weekly after-school programs and monthly mother-daughter workshops.

The majority of the girls who will participate in the coming school year are already members of *Jump Start Girls! Adelante Ninas!* The program will build on the relationships, trust and motivation already established. New members will be added in 4th grade at both elementary schools, and 5th, 6th, and 7th grades where there are openings.

All participants are recommended by their guidance counselor or teacher based on a set of criteria that may indicate risk, such as talented but disinterested in school, low self-esteem, poor communication and negotiation skills, precocious sexual development, physical traits that cause embarrassment, poor attendance, girls from immigrant families, or girls who have an interest in gangs.

Each two and one-half hour weekly meeting focuses on one of six themes and is geared toward creating a strong, supportive team of students and adult team leaders. The relationships that are built within and across culture, race, and age in each team are essential to achieving our goals. We use critical thinking and the arts to develop self-confidence, self-expression, and analytic skills. Girls are encouraged to speak out, to take on new challenges, to value and respect one another, and to assume responsibility within the group, in their school, and in the community.

A grant of $10,000 from the Meyer Foundation will enable Community Bridges to hire a social worker part-time in order to increase counseling and advocacy for students and outreach to families. With the addition of a social worker to our staff, we will pursue the following program goals for the coming year:

- Continue to develop a multicultural, feminist empowerment and leadership development curriculum that will be a model for other organizations.
- Develop an approach to community action that is integrated into the curriculum throughout the year and leads to student-initiated projects.
- Engage more mentors and volunteers in every aspect of our program and hire an additional youth worker.
- Build a teen advisory group.
- Increase our efforts to build bridges among community agencies, cultural organizations, businesses, local universities and community colleges, and public schools.
- Develop the peer mentoring and mediation component of the 6th and 7th grade curriculum.

Neither example contains every element of the ideal executive summary, but both persuasively present the case for reading further.

4

Developing the Master Proposal: The Statement of Need

If the funder reads beyond the executive summary, you have successfully piqued his or her interest. Your next task is to build on this initial interest in your project by enabling the funder to understand the problem that the project will remedy.

The statement of need will enable the reader to learn more about the issues. It presents the facts and evidence that support the need for the project and establishes that your nonprofit understands the problems and therefore can reasonably address them. The information used to support the case can come from authorities in the field, as well as from your agency's own experience.

You want the need section to be succinct, yet persuasive. Like a good debater, you must assemble all the arguments and then present them in a logical sequence that will readily convince the reader of their importance. As you marshal your arguments, consider the following six points:

First, decide which facts or statistics best support the project. Be sure the data you present are accurate. There are few things more embarrassing than to have the funder tell you that your information is out of date or incorrect. Information that is too generic or broad will not help you develop a winning argument for your project. Information that does not relate to your organization or the project you are presenting will cause the funder to question the entire proposal. There should be a balance between the information presented and the scale of the program.

An example might be helpful here. Your nonprofit organization plans to initiate a program for battered women, for which you will seek support from foundations and corporations in your community. You have impressive national statistics on hand. You can also point to an increasing number of local women and their children seeking help. However, local data is limited. Given the scope of the project and the base of potential supporters, you should probably use the more limited local information only. It is far more relevant to the interest of funders close to home. If you were to seek support from more nationally oriented funders, then the broader information would be helpful, supplemented by details based on local experience.

Second, give the reader hope. The picture you paint should not be so grim that the situation appears hopeless. The funder will wonder whether an investment in a solution will be worthwhile. Here's an example of a solid statement of need: "Breast cancer kills. But statistics prove that regular check-ups catch most breast cancer in the early stages, reducing the likelihood of death. Hence, a program to encourage preventive checkups will reduce the risk of death due to breast cancer." Avoid overstatement and overly emotional appeals.

Third, decide if you want to put your project forward as a model. This could expand the base of potential funders, but serving as a model works only for certain types of projects. Don't try to make this argument if it doesn't really fit. Funders may well expect your agency to follow through with a replication plan if you present your project as a model.

If the decision about a model is affirmative, you should document how the problem you are addressing occurs in other communities.

Be sure to explain how your solution could be a solution for others as well.

Fourth, determine whether it is reasonable to portray the need as acute. You are asking the funder to pay attention to your proposal because either the problem you address is worse than others or the solution you propose makes more sense than others. Here is an example of a balanced but weighty statement: "Drug abuse is a national problem. Each day, children all over the country die from drug overdose. In the South Bronx the problem is worse. More children die here than any place else. It is an epidemic. Hence, our drug prevention program is needed more in the South Bronx than in any other part of the city."

Fifth, decide whether you can demonstrate that your program addresses the need differently or better than other projects that preceded it. It is often difficult to describe the need for your project without being critical of the competition. But you must be careful not to do so. Being critical of other nonprofits will not be well received by the funder. It may cause the funder to look more carefully at your own project to see why you felt you had to build your case by demeaning others. The funder may have invested in these other projects or may begin to consider them, now that you have brought them to its attention.

If possible, you should make it clear that you are cognizant of, and on good terms with, others doing work in your field. Keep in mind that today's funders are very interested in collaboration. They may even ask why you are not collaborating with those you view as key competitors. So at the least you need to describe how your work complements, but does not duplicate, the work of others.

Sixth, avoid circular reasoning. In circular reasoning, you present the absence of your solution as the actual problem. Then your solution is offered as the way to solve the problem. For example, the circular reasoning for building a community swimming pool might go like this: "The problem is that we have no pool in our community. Building a pool will solve the problem." A more persuasive case would cite what a pool has meant to a neighboring community, permitting it to offer recreation, exercise, and physical therapy programs. The statement might refer to a survey that underscores the target audience's planned usage of the facility and conclude with the connection between the proposed usage and potential benefits to enhance life in the community.

The statement of need does not have to be long and involved. Short, concise information captures the reader's attention. This is the case in the following example from a proposal by WomenVenture to the General Mills Foundation.

The Need

According to the Department of Economic Security, Minnesota's unemployment rate has remained below the three-percent level since November 1997, dipping to a record 2.3 percent in December 1999 (seasonally adjusted). The economy is booming, and employers are struggling to find enough workers to meet business demand.

In spite of these positive growth signs, Minnesota's economy is not generating sufficient jobs for welfare recipients and low-skilled, unemployed workers. Neighborhood sources such as the Urban Coalition and JOBS NOW Coalition estimate unemployment as high as 27 percent in the inner cities, where approximately 65 percent of welfare recipients live. This is a logistical problem, since fewer than 32 percent of available jobs are located in the inner cities (Minnesota Department of Economic Security).

In addition, a significant portion of Minnesota's underemployed and unemployed population has neither the skills nor the support systems to become economically self-sufficient. Yet some welfare-to-work clients are taking minimum-wage jobs before they complete training programs as a hedge against losing current welfare benefits. This short-term choice perpetuates poverty and undermines clients in achieving their long-term goal of economic self-sufficiency by way of a livable-wage income.

Traditional jobs for minimally skilled, low-income individuals—and particularly for women—do not pay livable wages. One strategy for breaking poverty cycles is to train women for nontraditional occupations that pay higher wages, such as those in the cable installation, construction, and printing industries. Another strategy is to equip individuals who want to own their own businesses with the knowledge, support, and capital to achieve their goal.

The barriers low-income individuals encounter can make their journey to self-sufficiency extremely difficult. Some barriers are linked to individual histories, such as low levels of education and experience, limited knowledge about livable-wage jobs, unstable housing, domestic abuse, and low self-esteem. Other client barriers are systemic, and include the following:

- Women fill a very small number of jobs in nontraditional occupations that pay livable wages, such as cable installation, construction, or printing.

- In some settings, there is significant bias against welfare recipients, based on stereotypical assumptions.

- In spite of limited resources, women have major expenses related to work, including but not limited to childcare, transportation, clothing, tools, and union dues.

In order to best serve these clients, it is vitally important to develop a network of strategic partnerships so that the continuum of service is seamless. Many years of serving clients has revealed that a one-stop shop for services is what clients most need and desire. WomenVenture is acutely aware of this need, and the agency continues to move purposefully in this direction.

The next example comes from a proposal to the Eugene and Agnes E. Meyer Foundation submitted by Community Bridges. Since this is a request from a local agency to a grantmaker based in the same geographic area, the need section relies appropriately on local data and information.

Purpose of the Grant

Needs and Problems: *Jump Start Girls! Adelante Ninas!* addresses a critical need in East Silver Spring and Takoma Park, Maryland for prevention and empowerment programs specifically designed for early adolescent girls and their mothers. According to a fall 1997 Community Bridges' survey of youth-serving agencies and schools, no youth development program specifically attempted to empower underserved girls ages 9–15, or to assist them with the often difficult elementary-middle school transition. Our project was created to ensure the academic success, social and emotional well-being, and safety of young girls in this community.

Quebec Terrace/Carroll Avenue and Flower Avenue/Piney Branch Road are high crime neighborhoods where many families manage on very low incomes, in many cases in crowded and substandard housing. Public health workers and local community agencies have been concerned about gang activity, teen prostitution, out-of-school and out-of-work immigrant youth, and the susceptibility of the population to HIV/AIDS and other health risks.

Immigrant families may not stay long in this community as they seek safer neighborhoods, better work, and better housing. Thus, continuity in schooling and in relationships is often disrupted. Furthermore, children whose parent(s) or guardian(s) work evenings or weekends spend long hours unsupervised at an early age. Many nine and ten year-old girls in *Jump Start Girls! Adelante Ninas!* have significant responsibilities as caretakers of younger siblings.

In early adolescence, girls need adult attention and a variety of opportunities to explore in safe and healthy ways. This critical stage of development can be even more challenging for girls from families struggling to meet basic needs and when young people are quickly becoming bicultural and bilingual, and their parents are not. Girls are particularly vulnerable to diminished academic achievement, drop-out, pregnancy, sexual and physical abuse, low self-esteem, and depression.

A final example is from a proposal submitted by the Madison School District to the Flinn Foundation. It makes effective use of both an emotionally charged quotation and compelling statistics.

Statement of Need

"No child can escape his community. . . . The life of the community flows about him, foul or pure; he swims in it, goes to sleep in it, and wakes to the new day to find it still about him. He belongs to it; it nourishes him, or starves him, or poisons him; it gives him the substance of his life." —J. K. Hart

It is this very reason that the Madison Schools seek to expand our HIV/AIDS education program into the community that our children belong to.

Quarterly, the Arizona Department of Health Services' Summary on HIV/AIDS is published showing the devastating effects of this virus on Arizona's people. In particular, it brings to full attention the incidents of infection. In the report dated ____, there were 35 AIDS cases of children under 19 years, 759 cases in the 20–29 age category, and 1,695 cases of AIDS in the 30–39 age group in the state. It has been clearly expressed that the virus can be dormant for up to 15 years, so it is obvious that these figures indicate that teenagers are contracting this virus, and its outcome is showing in the 20–40 age group. Education must start early, before teens reach the age of "experimentation and know-it-all sophistication."

In looking at teen HIV infection, there are 56 reported asymptomatic cases in the state, with 38 of these in Maricopa County. In the same age group, there are five sympotomic HIV cases in the state, with four of these in our county. Based on the zip codes that make up our own school district (85020, 85016, 85014, 85013, and 85012), we find that there is only one zip code in the entire county with an equal incidence of reported HIV cases to our own district attendance area (Exhibit A). This is alarming news to us as we ponder ways in which we can be more effective in educating our students and our community. The data shows we are not doing all that we must to educate our community. We must expand what we're already doing!

As you can see from all three examples, the need statement begins the process whereby the organization builds its case and tells its story. This process continues in the next section of the proposal, which describes how the project will address the need.

5

Developing the
Master Proposal:
The Project Description

In this section, describe the nuts and bolts of the project in a way that gets the reader excited about it, while making a compelling case for the approach you have adopted. It is worth stating right up front that your plan is not written in stone. It might change based on feedback on your proposal and the experience you gain through implementation. It is not worth putting your organization in a defensive position in negotiating with grantmakers, and you certainly don't want to surprise a funder if in the project's final report, you state that you changed your approach.

This section of your proposal should have five subsections: objectives, methods, staffing/administration, evaluation, and sustainability. Together, objectives and methods dictate staffing and administrative requirements. They then become the focus of the evaluation to assess the results of the project. The project's sustainability flows directly from its success, hence its ability to attract other support. The five subsections present an interlocking picture of the total project.

Objectives

Objectives are the measurable outcomes of the program. They help delineate your methods. Your objectives must be tangible, specific, concrete, measurable, and achievable in a specified time period. Grantseekers often confuse objectives with goals, which are conceptual and more abstract. For the purpose of illustration, here is the goal of a project with a subsidiary objective:

Goal: Our afterschool program will help children read better.

Objective: Our afterschool remedial education program will assist 50 children in improving their reading scores by one grade level as demonstrated on standardized reading tests administered after participating in the program for six months.

The goal in this case is abstract: improving reading, while the objective is much more specific. It is achievable in the short term (six months) and measurable (improving 50 children's reading scores by one grade level).

With competition for dollars so great, well-articulated objectives are increasingly critical to a proposal's success.

Calling upon a different example, there are at least four types of objectives:

1. Behavioral—A human action is anticipated.
   Example: Fifty of the 70 children participating will learn to swim.

2. Performance—A specific time frame within which a behavior will occur, at an expected proficiency level, is anticipated.
   Example: Fifty of the 70 children will learn to swim within six months and will pass a basic swimming

proficiency test administered by a Red Cross–certified lifeguard.

3. Process—The manner in which something occurs is an end in itself.
   Example: We will document the teaching methods utilized, identifying those with the greatest success.

4. Product—A tangible item will result.
   Example: A manual will be created to be used in teaching swimming to this age and proficiency group in the future.

In any given proposal, you will find yourself setting forth one or more of these types of objectives, depending on the nature of your project. Be certain to present the objectives very clearly. Make sure that they do not become lost in verbiage and that they stand out on the page. You might, for example, use numbers, bullets, or indentations to denote the objectives in the text. Above all, be realistic in setting objectives. Don't promise what you can't deliver. Remember, the funder will want to be told in the final report that the project actually accomplished these objectives.

The example that follows is from a proposal to the Henry Luce Foundation from the San Francisco Theological Seminary. It is a brief statement of the proposed project's objectives, presented in outline form.

Expected Outcomes

With partnership support from The Henry Luce Foundation, San Francisco Theological Seminary looks forward to the following:

A. An established network for recruiting students, financial contributions, and other forms of support for the Seminary in Southern California from among its diverse constituencies.

B. An increase in SFTS/SC student enrollment by 100 percent by academic year 2004, reflecting the breadth of racial/ethnic and cultural constituencies in the region.

C. A carefully developed and secure funding base for SFTS/SC and its programs within the overall Seminary community, as demonstrated by a 20 percent yearly increase in the SFTS Annual Giving campaign resulting from new individual donors in Southern California.

D. A refined system of delivering theological education in multilingual settings, balancing the needs of those training for church leadership today with the needs of congregations of the future. Some experimentation with techniques of translation, tutoring in "theological English," distance learning, and the like will occur.

E. The continued evolution of a creative curriculum for training church leaders especially geared to service in a multicultural urban context. This will include the SFTS emphasis on spiritual formation and solid grounding in stewardship education. We seek a careful balance between theological understanding and disciplines and the practical skills for ministry that will equip leaders for the church of the future.

Another example is from the Madison School District proposal. It delivers a clear statement of objectives for a project.

Purpose and Goals

To address the needs described in the previous section, this project will achieve the following purpose and goals:

Purpose

The purpose of this project is to take the Madison School District HIV/AIDS education program to the logical next step by integrating with our 7th and 8th grade curriculum across the board and expanding the knowledge base of our professional staff and community.

During the planning period for which funding is requested, our proposed project will target the following goals:

Goals

I. Integrate HIV instruction in all areas of the curriculum by building a model that could be used in math, literature, writing, science, social studies, and life skills. This would expand HIV/AIDS classroom instruction over a period of six weeks from the current two hours in 7th and 8th grade.

II. Extend teacher training to ensure positive attitudes and commitment to the goal of HIV education.

III. Promote parent/family education, which would allow noted speakers to address student behavior, media impact on our adolescents, and skills to provide the courage to say "no" as teens begin their journey into adulthood. Central to this project is the basic premise that parents, in any culture or situation, have the greatest influence and opportunity to teach HIV infection prevention to their children.

These three goals, when fully achieved, will provide for an integrated, in-depth HIV/AIDS curriculum, which is meaningful to our students and integrated in the healthy lifestyle of our community.

Methods

By means of the objectives, you have explained to the funder what will be achieved by the project. The methods section describes the specific activities that will take place to achieve the objectives. It might be helpful to divide our discussion of methods into the following: how, when, and why.

How: This is the detailed description of what will occur from the time the project begins until it is completed. Your methods should match the previously stated objectives. In our example about teaching 50 children to swim, appropriate methods would describe: 1) how the youngsters will be recruited, 2) how they will be taught to enhance their skills, and 3) how their swimming skills will be measured. There would be no reason to describe an extraneous activity like helping the parents learn to enjoy swimming with their children, because using swimming to bring the family together in wholesome exercise is not a stated objective of the project.

The Community Projects Foundation proposal to the John S. and James L. Knight Foundation briefly describes an audience development project.

The CPF requests funding to conduct and implement a collaborative audience research and development effort among the organizations involved in the Challenge that can also act as a model for similar organizations in small- to mid-sized cities. In addition to the CPF, the nine organizations involved are: the Coca-Cola Space Science Center, the Columbus Museum, the Columbus Symphony Orchestra, the Historic Columbus Foundation, the Liberty Theatre Cultural Center, Port Columbus Civil War Naval Center, the RiverCenter for the Performing Arts, the Schwob Department of Music of Columbus State University, and the Springer Opera House. This project is not unlike the efforts being taken by the collaborative efforts in Long Beach and San Jose, California, and we will share information with these communities.

This project involves three phases: audience research, marketing plan development, and plan implementation. Knight funds are being requested to make possible the first and second phases, which will be carried out by a market research firm specializing in research and marketing counseling for arts, culture, and history organizations.

Phase One consists of a thorough analysis of the existing and potential arts, culture, and history audiences in our area and, for organizations whose audience might be primarily tourist visitors, outside our area. The analysis will involve both general research and research specific to each organization. Phase Two consists of the development of marketing plans for each organization, identifying every possible avenue for collaborative efforts among one or more of the other participating organizations. Phase Three, the implementation phase, will implement, for purposes of this project, only the collaborative efforts identified in Phase Two. Components of each group's plan that are specific only to that group will be carried out on a funds-available basis at the discretion of the group, outside of this project.

Implementation of the project will probably take 24 months, broken down as follows: three months to identify and hire the consulting firm, six months for them to design and conduct their research, two months for them to design and present their marketing plans, and 12 months for the organizations to implement the resulting collaborative marketing efforts. In addition to regular evaluation meetings among the organization principals during the project period, at the conclusion of the project, one month of follow-up evaluation will be conducted, and a case study will be written and submitted to Knight Foundation.

In addition to the case study prepared for Knight Foundation, results and conclusions of the project will be shared with other arts, culture, and history groups in our area, involving each of them in efforts to offer services to a maximum number of people as well as other Knight communities.

Another application to the Knight Foundation from the Museum of Science in Boston, Massachusetts, lays out detailed plans for a touring exhibit. For the sake of brevity, we have shortened it here.

The Museum of Science is planning, developing, and implementing a major new interdisciplinary traveling exhibition entitled *The Secrets of Aging*, which examines the processes and effects of human aging from scientific, social, humanistic, and cultural perspectives. *The Secrets of Aging* is scheduled to open at the Museum of Science in April 2000, and it will tour nationally (the tour will include the *Journey with Me* component) during the following three years to the other five museums making up the Science Museum Exhibit Collaborative. After that time, the exhibition will be available to travel to additional sites. Two of the six SMEC museums to which the exhibition will travel are located in Knight communities of interest: The Franklin Institute in Philadelphia and the Science Museum of Minnesota in St. Paul; a third museum directly serves a Knight community of interest: the California Science Center in Los Angeles, which serves Long Beach; and a fourth museum, the Center of Science and Industry, is within 125 miles of the Knight community of interest of Akron, Ohio.

The general purpose of the exhibition is to explore the most recent findings and research about aging and to look at how aging is interpreted by a wide range of cultures and individuals. One component of this exhibition is a multimedia piece entitled *Journey with Me: Stories of Growing Older,* which is a compilation of narrative stories and experiences related to the aging process, as told by individuals from different backgrounds and cultures. The narratives will be overlaid onto a variety of visual and aural effects, including an interpretive, intergenerational dance/movement piece choreographed specifically in conjunction with the narratives. *Journey with Me: Stories of Growing Older* will be installed within *The Secrets of Aging* as a conceptual centerpiece of the overall exhibition experience, helping to merge the personal and humanistic aspects of the subject of aging with the scientific aspects.

While *The Secrets of Aging* exhibition as a whole will look comprehensively at physical changes associated with aging, the social and psychological impact of aging, and myths and attitudes about the aging process, *Journey with Me: Stories of Growing Older* will widen the scope with a personal touch presented in a multimedia, oral history format. *Stories of Growing Older* will incorporate personal reflections of those who are aging, and they will strike a balance between the state of mind and the state of body of aging people. And in keeping with the general theme of the exhibition, this component will also include examples of aging with dignity and grace.

The multimedia piece *Journey with Me: Stories of Growing Older* is the specific component of the *Secrets of Aging* exhibition for which the Museum of Science is requesting funding from the John S. and James L. Knight Foundation. *Journey with Me* is a multimedia experience that will be a centerpiece of the exhibition and is critical to making *The Secrets of Aging* a well-rounded experience for visitors. With its focus on individual experience, it will serve as contrast, counterpoint, and reinforcement to some of the other elements of the exhibition. The mix of humanistic, scientific, social, and cultural contexts make *The Secret of Aging* a very ambitious exhibition but also one that can be extremely rewarding to museum visitors.

The work to create *Journey with Me: Stories of Growing Older* will be a collaboration among a writer/exhibit developer, a videographer, a choreographer and dancers, photographers, musicians, the storytellers, and technical people. The Liz Lerman Dance Exchange has been selected to work with the Museum because of Ms. Lerman's renowned work with life stories, older dancers, and intergenerational dance. Roberta Cooks, the writer/developer for this piece, has also used life stories extensively in developing major traveling and permanent exhibits for museums on subjects including *The Brain*, *AIDS*, and *The Powers of Nature*. The *Journey with Me* component, in all its facets, will act as an exhibit centerpiece that conveys the drama, humor, and enormous possibilities for growth and change as we age.

Think about how you can most readily construct a logical sequence from each objective to its relevant method. This can be accomplished in a number of ways, some relating simply to visual placement on the page.

One means of organizing this section is to write out each objective and to list beneath it the method(s) that will make the objective possible. For example, it might look like this:

Objective: to recruit 70 children

Methods:

- Put up signs in the Y.
- Go to each school and address classes on the fun of swimming.
- Put ads in the local paper.
- Enclose a flyer about the program with the next mailer sent out to each family in the community.

The methods should match the magnitude of the objectives. Once you are sure that each objective has related methods that describe how the objective will be achieved, you should check that the emphasis given each method matches the importance of the related objective. In our swimming example, recruitment of 70 children is probably the least important objective; demonstrating that 50 of them can pass the Red Cross test is more critical. To match the magnitude of the objectives with appropriate detail about the project, more emphasis should be placed on the testing than on recruiting.

(This refining and highlighting of information will enable the reader to understand the project and to have confidence in your agency.)

The methods should appear doable; otherwise, you lose credibility. For example, if the swimming course is to be taught by an Olympic swimmer who remains anonymous, the reader might question whether the organization can deliver what it has promised. However, if the Olympic star is identified by name and has already agreed to run the program, the reader will likely be convinced.

When: The methods section should present the order and timing for the various tasks. It might make sense to provide a timetable so that the reader does not have to map out the sequencing on his or her own. The timetable could look like this one, excerpted from a proposal to the Henry Luce Foundation from the Louisville Seminary.

Time Line

If this grant is approved, we will pursue the following time line:

July 2000:

- The Dean will hire writing and ESL tutors.

August–September 2000:

- Dean of Students Donna Melloan, Director of Vocational Formation Garnett Foster, and Interim Dean of the Seminary and Director of Graduate Studies Dianne Reistroffer will coordinate orientation and testing of entering students in all masters-level degree programs.

September 2000–May 2001

- Search started for Director of Academic Support Services by February, with appointment made by the President.
- The Dean and the faculty will plan and conduct two faculty seminars on topics identified in the grant and/or the faculty planning team.

- Area A faculty will develop language preparatory courses for Hebrew and Greek for implementation during academic year 2001–2002.

- The Dean of the Seminary and the Dean of Students, in consultation with the faculty (especially Area A Faculty), will identify the ten to twelve students who will require financial support during the summer language prep course and the Hebrew class.

- In consultation with the English Department at the University of Louisville and the Louisville Seminary faculty, the Dean will develop and implement a provisional Writing Lab and *Writing Helps* program.

- In consultation with the Education Department at the University of Louisville and the Louisville Seminary faculty, the Dean will develop and implement a provisional testing program for students with learning disabilities and secure community-based resources to develop individual, adaptive-educational plans for seminary students with learning disabilities.

- Preparations begun for the PC (USA) Consultation on Academic Readiness in Theological Education (tentatively scheduled for Fall 2001).

June 2001–May 2002

- Language preparatory courses implemented.

- Conduct PC (USA) Consultation (September or October 2001).

- Other programs implemented as in previous years, with expected modifications of the *Writing Helps* and Learning Disabilities Support programs by the new Director of Academic Support Services.

- Plan and conduct ATS Workshop (Spring 2002).

- First evaluation of the program submitted to the faculty and Board of Trustees in April 2002.

June 2002–May 2003

- Programs changed as necessary, after evaluation. Implementation continues.
- Final evaluation of the program under grant funding submitted to the faculty and the Board of Trustees in April 2003.

Another presentation of a solid work plan comes from a proposal submitted to the Flinn Foundation by the Hualapai Tribal Health Department. The timeline depicts a one-year project.

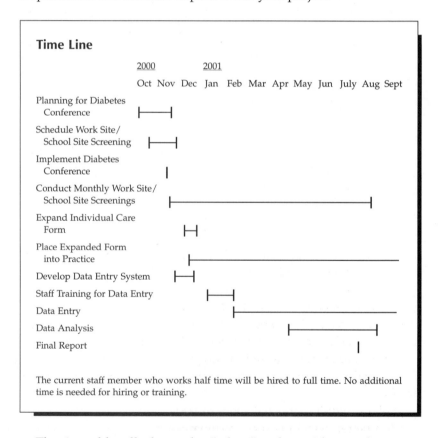

Time Line

	2000			2001								
	Oct	Nov	Dec	Jan	Feb	Mar	Apr	May	Jun	July	Aug	Sept
Planning for Diabetes Conference	⊢—⊣											
Schedule Work Site/ School Site Screening		⊢—⊣										
Implement Diabetes Conference				⎮								
Conduct Monthly Work Site/ School Site Screenings				⊢—————————————⊣								
Expand Individual Care Form			⊢—⊣									
Place Expanded Form into Practice				⊢—————————————————								
Develop Data Entry System			⊢—⊣									
Staff Training for Data Entry				⊢—⊣								
Data Entry				⊢—————————————								
Data Analysis						⊢————⊣						
Final Report										⎮		

The current staff member who works half time will be hired to full time. No additional time is needed for hiring or training.

The timetable tells the reader "when" and provides another summary of the project that supports the rest of the methods section.

Why: You need to defend your chosen methods, especially if they are new or unorthodox. Why will the planned work lead to the outcomes you anticipate? You can answer this question in a number of ways, including using examples of other projects that work and expert testimony.

The methods section enables the reader to visualize the implementation of the project. It should convince the reader that your agency knows what it is doing, thereby establishing credibility.

Staffing/Administration

In describing the methods, you will have mentioned staffing for the project. You now need to devote a few sentences to discussing the number of staff, their qualifications, and specific assignments. Details about individual staff members involved in the project can be included either as part of this section or in the appendix, depending on the length and importance of this information.

"Staffing" can refer to volunteers or to consultants, as well as to paid staff. Most proposal writers do not develop staffing sections for projects that are primarily volunteer-run. Describing tasks that volunteers will undertake, however, can be most helpful to the proposal reader. Such information underscores the value added by the volunteers and the cost-effectiveness of the project.

For a project with paid staff, be certain to describe which staff will work full time and which will work part time on the project. Identify staff already employed by your nonprofit and those to be recruited specifically for the project. How will you free up the time of an already fully deployed individual?

Salary and project costs are affected by the qualifications of the staff. Delineate the practical experience you require for key staff, as well as level of expertise and educational background. If an individual has already been selected to direct the program, summarize his or her credentials and include a brief biographical sketch in the appendix. A strong project director can help influence a grant decision.

Explain anything unusual about the proposed staffing for the project. It is better to include such information in the proposal narrative than to have the funder raise questions once the proposal review begins.

Three samples of staffing sections follow. The first is part of a proposal submitted by Alternatives for Community & Environment to the Hyams Foundation. It describes a complex arrangement of staff, board, and volunteers.

Staff

ACE has eight staff, including the Executive Director, Research & Development Director, two Staff Attorneys, Community Organizer, Program Director, Office Director/Community Organizer, and Communications Coordinator. ACE has a relatively flat staff structure, with each staff member taking on a high degree of responsibility and participation in organizational decision making. Currently, every staff person is involved in some program work. Senior management decisions are made by the Executive Director and the Research & Development Director. The two Staff Attorneys provide legal support, and each also coordinates one of ACE's programs. The Community Organizer and the Program Director are co-directors of REEP. The Office Director/Community Organizer is our bookkeeper and office manager as well as an organizer in our initiatives. The Communications Coordinator provides support to all the programs, including maintaining the contact database and all public materials and publishing our newsletter.

In addition to the regular staff, ACE has a number of paid interns. Over the course of the year, these include four-six local high school youth who work with REEP, two summer interns who support programs, and two-three legal interns. There is a growing number of volunteer interns as well, including approximately another ten local youth, a dozen residents, and four college and graduate students.

ACE's Board of Directors has eleven members, who meet four times a year for official business and who remain actively involved in supporting ACE throughout the year (see below). The Greater Boston Environmental Justice Network is overseen by the GBEJN Steering Committee ("SC"). The SC is predominantly led and overseen by women from community organizations. The Steering Committee, elected at the founding conference, consists of eleven seats, including representatives of various neighborhoods and organizations and youth. This structure is key in providing accountability to the larger membership and ensuring that their concerns and ideas are addressed in the actions of the Network as a whole. In addition, ACE maintains advisory committees for REEP and the MEJN that consist of our community partners and allies. Advisory committees help ACE assess performance and provide input on annual work plans and our strategic plan.

In ACE's seven years of existence, we have had a total of thirteen staff, including the current eight. The co-founders left ACE as Co-Directors but moved to the Board of Directors. ACE's first Executive Director left after eighteen months after an offer of a high-level position at the state's Executive Office of Environmental Affairs. ACE's first Staff Attorney left after almost three years of employment, but also serves on our Board. Only one staff position turned over in under a year.

ACE has a corps of volunteers which includes the members of the MEJN and, on an annual basis, approximately seven legal interns, four college and graduate school students, and ten local youth. We commit the most resources to our youth volunteers, whom we encourage to take an active role in our work, to gain real organizing skills and other experiences, which help prepare them for the job market.

ACE strives to be representative of the communities it works with, in terms of race, gender, economic class, and age. In the long term, we are committed to hiring those who are from the communities we work in, especially the youth who have been involved with ACE. Of ACE's eight staff members, two are African American, two are Asian American/Pacific Islander, and four are white. Five are women. Three reside in our constituent communities. The eleven-member Board includes two community activists, seven attorneys, one academic administrator, and one youth representative. Seven members of the Board are people of color, five are women, and ten are from the Boston area.

Our commitment to empowerment began by locating Boston's poorest neighborhood of color, to be closer and more accessible to our primary constituency. In seven years, we have successfully built a diverse and extremely talented staff, including attorneys, community organizers, environmental scientists, and administrative staff. All staff take full part in the strategic planning and decision making. And particularly for those staff from the neighborhoods we work with, we have supported skills development and advancement within the organization. For example, Klare Allen, a formerly homeless mother of four, was initially hired as community organizer and after three years was promoted to Co-Director of the program she works on. Khalida Smalls, a single mother who is raising her four-year-old son in the Roxbury and Dorchester neighborhood where she grew up, began at ACE as an administrative assistant. She now coordinates the Greater Boston Environmental Justice Network and is planning to return to college to pursue environmental studies and complete her degree.

See attachments for staff biographies.

The Community Bridges proposal provides a simple, straightforward staffing section.

Staff: Naomi Nim, Ed.D., Executive Director, is a multicultural educator and nonprofit manager with expertise in the arts, cross-cultural communication, and conflict resolution. She works part-time as Director of Education and Training at CASA of Maryland (resume attached). Aisha Cooper, Youthworker, is a senior at the University of Maryland College Park pursuing a degree in Family Studies and Human Development with an emphasis on public policy. She is a talented artist and performer. Ms. Cooper immigrated to the United States from Liberia as a child and grew up in Baltimore, where she became a youth leader of Sisters In The Spirit. Upon graduation Ms. Cooper plans to become an AmeriCorps volunteer and to attend graduate school in public policy.

Finally, the Center for Responsive Politics presents information about the board as well as key staff.

An active Board of Directors guides the Center's work. This board is led by two former members of Congress: Senator Dick Clark and Representative Orval Hansen. Until recently, Senator Hugh Scott, a founder of the Center, has also lent his considerable leadership and expertise to the Center. Other members of the Board include individuals with distinguished public service careers: Bethine Church, Peter Fenn, George Denison, Paul Hoff, Steven Hofman, Paul Thomas, Robert A. Weinberger and Executive Director Ellen Miller, as well as philanthropist Peter Kovler, and public relations executive Tim Brosnahan.

The Center's Executive Director—Ellen Miller—has extensive congressional experience, both as a senior staffer in both the House and Senate, and as a veteran of the public interest community in Washington. As Executive Director of the Center for Responsive Politics, she directs and manages all project areas: Money and Politics, Congressional Operations, Congress and the Media, Ethics in Government, and Foundations in Public Policy. In addition, as the Center's Executive Director for the past six years, she has been responsible for providing overall management, program planning, direction and fundraising and outreach for the organization.

The Center's Senior Research Associate—Larry Makinson—will serve as Project Director for this project. One of the pioneers of computer research on campaign financing, he is the author of four books on the subject, including *Open Secrets: The Dollar Power of PACs in Congress* and *The Price of Admission: An Illustrated Atlas of Campaign Spending in the 1988 Congressional Elections*. As a longtime journalist in Alaska, Makinson won national awards for his reporting both in newspapers and public television. He holds a masters degree in public administration from the Kennedy School of Government at Harvard University.

Describe for the reader your plans for administering the project. This is especially important in a large operation, if more than one agency is collaborating on the project, or if you are using a fiscal agent. It needs to be crystal clear who is responsible for financial management, project outcomes, and reporting.

Evaluation

An evaluation plan should not be considered only after the project is over; it should be built into the project. Including an evaluation plan in your proposal indicates that you take your objectives seriously and want to know how well you have achieved them. Evaluation is also a sound management tool. Like strategic planning, it helps a nonprofit refine and improve its program. To quote Charles Rooks of the Meyer Memorial Trust, "Evaluation is critical. It provides discipline for a grantee." An evaluation can often be the best means for others to learn from your experience in conducting the project.

Match the evaluation to the project. If you are asking for funds to buy an additional personal computer, it is not necessary to develop an elaborate plan to assess its impact on your operation. But if you have requested $100,000 to encourage people to have blood tests for Lyme disease, you should have a mechanism to determine whether the project's activities achieved your goals and objectives.

Many projects will have rather obvious evaluation procedures built into them. An art institution working on audience development, a settlement house providing an after-school program to disadvantaged children, or a health clinic offering preventive immunization will not spend a great deal of money and time evaluating their respective projects. The number of people served will be the major indicator of the success of these projects.

Not all funders require a formal evaluation; some want monitoring reports only. In this case, it is up to you to decide whether a formal evaluation is an essential component of the project. Many of the funders interviewed for this book, however, told us that a sound evaluation plan, based on measurable outcomes, is the hallmark of a successful proposal.

By way of an evaluation component, the Louisville Seminary excerpt cites specific outcomes.

Outcomes and Evaluations

1. By the fall of 2002, the retention rate of racial/ethnic/minority students and provisionally admitted students should improve by 50 percent, using figures from academic year 1998–1999 as a basis for comparison.

2. By the fall of 2003, 85 percent of those students who take Bible Content and other examinations for Presbyterian ordination will pass on the first attempt, using figures from academic year 1998–1999 as a basis of comparison. (57 percent passed Bible Content; 73 percent passed Theology; 75 percent passed Biblical Exegesis; 86 percent passed Polity; 97 percent passed Worship.)

3. By academic year 2003–2004, the enrollment of racial/ethnic/minority students will increase by 25 percent, using figures from academic year 1998–1999 as a basis for comparison.

4. Each year careful evaluation will be conducted with all students, faculty, and administrators who participate in programs sponsored by this grant. Qualitative and quantitative data will be gathered and assessed with these questions in mind:

   A. Perceived benefit to the overall educational mission of the seminary.

   B. Perceived benefit to students' well-being and success in seminary.

   C. Perceived benefit to seminary community life.

   D. Perceived impact on cultural diversity and affirmative action goals of the seminary.

   E. Perceived benefit to faculty.

   An advisory committee made up of the three area chairs, the student representative on the Academic Committee, the Director of Academic Support Services, the Dean of Students, and the Dean of the Seminary will oversee both the planning and implementation phases of these initiatives.

5. By academic year 2004–2005, at least four publications related to academic readiness in theological education will appear as a result of this program, including material presented at the PC (USA) Consultation in fall 2001 and the ATS workshop in spring 2002.

Here is the evaluation section of a proposal submitted by Heads Up to the Eugene and Agnes E. Meyer Foundation.

Evaluation Plan

At Heads Up we emphasize results and measure progress using standardized tests, individual reading inventories, and parent feedback. Our primary evaluation questions reflect this emphasis. They are:

- What percentage of participating students improved its reading skills at least one full grade level, as measured by diagnostic reading inventories?

- What percentage of participating students demonstrated improved attitudes, as measured by parents who report an "excellent" or "very good" change in end-of-year surveys?

- What percentage of students made gains on the reading portion of the Stanford 9 standardized test administered to DC public school students in the fall and spring of each school year?

- What percentage of students demonstrate more and/ or stronger peer connections? (*A task force of parents, students, and staff will determine the specific assessment method this summer.*)

These evaluation questions mirror the goals and outcomes of our programs as described earlier.

Our evaluation tools also include focus groups, student surveys, teacher feedback forms, and other indicators, including report cards and program attendance rates. In this way our rigorous program evaluation processes can also provide direction for our staff, identify training and technical assistance needs, point out program strengths and weaknesses, and suggest outcome targets.

This year we are studying how we measure our students' progress and AmeriCorps members' development and anticipate this work will yield additional ways of evaluating our programs next year. Specifically, we would like to have better tools to demonstrate the impact intense, sustained service and training in Heads Up has had on our members' intellectual, professional, and personal growth. Recent surveys revealed that 60 percent of Heads Up tutors and AmeriCorps members are now considering careers in teaching or public service as a result of the program. Seventy-five percent of these same undergraduates said that they were more likely to vote; 87 percent of them said they were more committed to improving the community.

The next excerpt is from a proposal The Field submitted to the Morgan Guaranty Trust Company of New York.

Measuring Effectiveness

The Field
Performance Zone Inc.

The Field measures its effectiveness much the same way an artist does: we must continue to seek increased exposure and growth without losing the creative spark that keeps us vital and responsive. Perhaps the strongest testament to our continued success is the many artists that are able to continue to return to us throughout many phases in their careers.

Participant and audience feedback on the effectiveness, relevance, and accessibility of our programming is an essential component of The Field's programming structure. Participants in our *Fieldwork* workshops are surveyed at the end of each session as to their experience in the program. In addition, all of our performance programs are "satisfaction guaranteed"; if an artist is not completely satisfied with her or his experience, we will refund the entire participation fee. The information we receive from artists helps us evaluate the programs we currently offer and develop new ones based on constituents' needs and ideas as they relate to New York City's ever-changing arts environment.

Last year, as part of our Board of Directors expansion, we added two rotating artist/constituent positions, who were nominated and elected by our member and constituent artists. These members offer insights on the executive level, helping us keep up with the changing demands and interests of the artists we serve. Finally, having developed a two-year plan in 1997, which focuses on the areas of Marketing and Dissemination, we will evaluate our progress based on those goals.

There are two types of formal evaluation. One measures the product; the other analyzes the process. Either or both might be appropriate to your project. The approach you choose will depend on the nature of the project and its objectives. For either type, you will need to describe the manner in which evaluative information will be collected and how the data will be analyzed. You should present your plan for how the evaluation and its results will be reported and the audiences to which it will be directed. For example, it might be used internally or be shared with the funder, or it might deserve a wider audience. A funder might have an opinion about the scope of this dissemination.

Should in-house staff or outside consultants conduct a formal evaluation? Staff may not have sufficient distance from the project to be objective. An outside person can bring objectivity to the project, but consultants may be costly and require time to learn about your agency and the project. Again, the nature of the project and of the evaluation may well determine the answer to this question. In any case, the evaluation section needs to strike a balance between familiarity with the project and objectivity about the product or process.

Sustainability

A clear message from grantmakers today is that grantseekers will be expected to demonstrate in very concrete ways the long-term financial viability of the project to be funded and of the nonprofit organization itself. Peter Bird of the Frist Foundation has this to say: "Sustainability is the Achilles heel in many proposals. The organization paints itself into a corner and then goes to the grantmaker for help. I have seen so many problems in the past."

It stands to reason that most grantmakers will not want to take on a permanent funding commitment to a particular agency. Rather, funders will want you to prove either that your project is finite (with start-up and ending dates); or that it is capacity-building (that it will contribute to the future self-sufficiency of your agency and/or enable it to expand services that might be revenue generating); or that it will make your organization attractive to other funders in the future. With the new trend toward adopting some of the investment principles of venture capital groups to the practice of philanthropy, evidence of fiscal sustainability becomes a highly sought-after characteristic of the successful grant proposal.

It behooves you to be very specific about current and projected funding streams, both earned income and fundraised, and about the base of financial support for your nonprofit. Here is an area where it is important to have backup figures and prognostications at the ready, in case a prospective funder asks for these, even though you are unlikely to include this information in the actual grant proposal. Some grantmakers, of course, will want to know who else will be receiving a copy of this same proposal. You should not be shy about sharing this information with the funder.

What follows is a brief statement regarding sustainability from the Community Bridges proposal to the Meyer Foundation.

> **Long-term Funding Strategies:** Community Bridges plans to strengthen its donor base through donor solicitation, a yearly dance benefit, and the efforts of an expanded and active Board to promote the organization in the community and to potential large donors. Community Bridges will be eligible to seek CDBG funding at substantial levels for the next two years and will be eligible to apply for a United Way grant this year. We will continue to actively pursue local foundation support and government funding sources at the state level.

And here's a post-grant funding plan submitted by the San Francisco Theological Seminary to the Henry Luce Foundation.

The Plan for Post-Grant Funding

To sustain SFTS/SC after completion of the grant, San Francisco Theological Seminary is taking the following steps:

A. Growth in the Seminary's Annual Giving Campaign, now exceeding 20 percent per year, will continue to result from new individual donors in Southern California. This will generate $391,000 a year in new gift income by 2003, permitting near self-sufficiency for SFTS/SC.

B. We will target SFTS/SC as a major component in a follow-on campaign to the Seminary's current highly successful capital campaign.

C. The institution's Director of Development position has been relocated to Southern California in order to oversee directly regional Annual Giving and major donor solicitation.

D. Because pastors need fundraising awareness in order to sustain and even expand their congregations, all students will have the opportunity to take the National Society of Fund Raising Executives' First Course on Fund Raising beginning January 1, 2001. All students will be encouraged to participate as volunteers in fundraising and to personally make planned gifts to the Seminary.

6

Developing the Master Proposal: The Budget

The project description provides the picture of your proposal in words. The budget further refines that picture with numbers. A well-crafted budget adds greatly to the proposal reviewer's understanding of your project.

The budget for your proposal may be as simple as a one-page statement of projected expenses. Or your proposal may require a more complex presentation, perhaps a spreadsheet including projected support and revenue and notes explaining various items of expense or revenue.

Expense Budget

As you prepare to assemble the budget, go back through the proposal narrative and make a list of all personnel and nonpersonnel items related to the operation of the project. Be sure that you list not only new costs that will be incurred if the project is funded but also any ongoing expenses for items that will be allocated to the project. Then get the relevant numbers from the person in your agency who is responsible for keeping the books. You may need to estimate the proportions of your agency's ongoing expenses that should be charged to the project and any new costs, such as salaries for project personnel not yet hired. Put the costs you have identified next to each item on your list.

It is accepted practice to include as line items in your project budget any operating costs of the agency that will be specifically devoted to running the project. Most commonly, these are the costs of supervision and of occupancy. If the project is large relative to the organization as a whole, these line items might also include telephone, utilities, office supplies, and computer-related expenses. For instance, if one of three office phone lines will be devoted to the project, one-third of the monthly cost of maintaining phone service could legitimately be listed as a project cost.

In addition, most expense budgets include a line called "overhead," which allows the project to bear a portion of the administrative costs, often called supporting services, of your operation. Such items as the bookkeeper's salary, board meeting expenses, the annual audit, and the cost of operating your personnel department might be included in the overhead figure. These costs are not directly attributable to the project but can be allocated to it based on the notion that the project should bear some of the costs of the host organization.

Most groups use a formula for allocating overhead costs to projects, usually based on the percentage of the total project budget to the total organizational budget or to its total salary line. For example, if the project budget is one-tenth the size of the total budget, it could be expected to bear one-tenth of the administrative overhead costs. Funders may have policies regarding the percentage of overhead that they will allow in a project budget. Some do not allow any overhead at all to be included. If possible, you should find out about the overhead policy before submitting your proposal to a particular foundation, because you may need to explain to that funder how you will cover overhead costs from other sources.

Your list of budget items and the calculations you have done to arrive at a dollar figure for each item should be summarized on worksheets. You should keep these to remind yourself how the numbers were developed. These worksheets can be useful as you continue to develop the proposal and discuss it with funders; they are also a valuable tool for monitoring the project once it is under way and for reporting after completion of the grant.

A portion of a worksheet for a year-long project might look like this:

Item	Description	Cost
Executive director	Supervision	10% of salary = $10,000 25% benefits = $2,500
Project director	Hired in month one	11 months full time at $35,000 = $32,083
Tutors	12 working 10 hours per week for 13 weeks	12 x 10 x 13 x $4.50 = $7,020
Office space	Requires 25% of current space	25% x $20,000 = $5,000
Overhead	20% of project cost	20% x $64,628 = $12,926

With your worksheets in hand, you are ready to prepare the expense budget. For most projects, costs should be grouped into subcategories, selected to reflect the critical areas of expense. All significant costs should be broken out within the subcategories, but small ones can be combined on one line. You might divide your expense budget into personnel and nonpersonnel costs. Personnel subcategories might include salaries, benefits, and consultants. Subcategories under nonpersonnel costs might include travel, equipment, and printing, for example, with a dollar figure attached to each line.

Two expense budgets follow. The first example, from a proposal submitted by the New York Botanical Garden to the Hyde and Watson Foundation, is for a relatively simple project, involving purchasing one piece of equipment.

The New York Botanical Garden
Plant Imaging Station
July 1, 1999 through June 30, 2000

Equipment Costs

Imaging Station	$52,060
Kodak DSC 66 Professional Camera	
Bencher Copy Stand	
Speedtron Strobe Lights	
Dell Precision 420 Workstation	
Computer	
Adobe Photoshop	
Accessories	5,146
Total Costs	$57,206
Total Expenditures	**$57,206**

The next budget, from the Madison School District, provides details on what the foundation is being asked to fund and what the school district itself will support.

BUDGET
YEAR ONE

	Flinn Fdn. Support	District In-Kind
A. PERSONNEL		
Professional Release Days		
12 days for 8th Grade Team & Project Director to plan and articulate	$ 600	
10 days for 10 teachers to attend AIDS workshops	$ 500	
4 days for Project Director to allow time to coordinate special speakers	$ 200	
Summer stipend for planning		
6 teachers—2 days each	$1,400	
Benefits at 13%	$ 82	
Summer curriculum integration workshop for 8th Grade Team		$ 3,000

	Flinn Fdn. Support	District In-Kind
.5 FTE Sex Ed Coordinator		$20,159
Benefits at 13%		
Clerical Personnel .10 FTE		$ 1,800
Benefits at 13%		$ 234

B. SUPPLIES AND MATERIALS

Professional Resources for 8th Grade Team including professional publications, student resource materials, and student literature	$1,000	
Library of materials available for parent and community checkout to support their work with their children	$1,500	
Audio visual material to support curriculum integration	$1,500	
Advertising materials to communicate activities to the community	$ 400	

C. CONTRACTUAL

Consultant fees for Parent Education and Study Groups	$1,000	
Speaker fees for community education and curriculum integration	$ 500	
Registration and travel fees for Project Director to attend the annual conference of the American Association of Sex Educators, Counselors and Therapists	$1,000	
Total	**$9,782**	**$25,193**

Support and Revenue Statement

For the typical project, no support and revenue statement is necessary. The expense budget represents the amount of grant support required. But if grant support has already been awarded to the project, or if you expect project activities to generate income, a support and revenue statement is the place to provide this information.

In itemizing grant support, make note of any earmarked grants; this will suggest how new grants may be allocated. The total grant support already committed should then be deducted from the "Total Expenses" line on the expense budget to give you the "Amount to Be Raised" or the "Balance Requested."

Any earned income anticipated should be estimated on the support and revenue statement. For instance, if you expect 50 people to attend your performance on each of the four nights, it is given at $10 a ticket, and if you hope that 20 of them will buy the $5 souvenir book each night, you would show two lines of income, "Ticket Sales" at $2,000 and "Souvenir Book Sales" at $400. As with the expense budget, you should keep backup worksheets for the support and revenue statement to remind yourself of the assumptions you have made.

Because an earned income statement deals with anticipated revenues, rather than grant commitments in hand, the difference between expenses and revenues is usually labeled "Balance Requested," rather than "Amount to Be Raised." The funder will appreciate your recognition that the project will earn even a small amount of money—and might well raise questions about this if you do not include it in your budget.

Now that your budget is complete, take the time to analyze it objectively. Be certain that the expense estimates are neither too lean nor on the high side. If you estimate too closely, you may not be able to operate within the budget. You will have to go back to funders already supporting the project for additional assistance, seek new donors, or underwrite part of the cost out of general operating funds. None of these alternatives is attractive.

Consistently overestimating costs can lead to other problems. The donor awards a grant expecting that all of the funds will support the project, and most will instruct you to return any funds remaining at the end. If you have a lot of money left over, it will reflect badly on your budgeting ability. This will affect the funder's receptiveness toward any future budgets you might present.

Finally, be realistic about the size of your project and its budget. You will probably be including a copy of the organization's financial statements in the appendix to your proposal. A red flag will be raised for the proposal reviewer if the budget for a new project rivals the size of the rest of your operation.

If you are inexperienced in developing proposal budgets, you should ask your treasurer or someone who has successfully managed grant funds to review it for you. This can help you spot obvious problems that need to be fixed, and it can prepare you to answer questions that proposal reviewers might raise, even if you decide not to change the budget.

Budget Narrative

A budget narrative portion is used to explain any unusual line items in the budget and is not always needed. If costs are straightforward and the numbers tell the story clearly, explanations are redundant.

If you decide a budget narrative is needed, you can structure it in one of two ways. You can create "Notes to the Budget," with footnote-style numbers on the line items in the budget keyed to numbered explanations. Or, if an extensive or more general explanation is required, you can structure the budget narrative as straight text. Remember, though, that the basic narrative about the project and your organization belong elsewhere in the proposal, not in the budget narrative.

The following is an example of a budget with an accompanying narrative from the Louisville Seminary. Note: this is a multi-year request.

BUDGET
Academic Support Services
Louisville Presbyterian Theological Seminary

ITEM	2000–2001	2001–2002	2002–2003
1. Personnel			
Dir. Academic Support Services			
Salary (50%)	0	23,507	24,179
Benefits (50%)	0	4,148	4,267
Work Study—Secretarial	0	6,000	6,000
Writing Tutors—2	12,000	12,000	12,000
2. Moving and Search Expenses	1,000	0	0
3. Office Equipment for 2 offices	12,000	0	0
4. Orientation and Testing of First-Year Students	5,000	5,500	6,000
5. Faculty Inservice Training/Materials and Speakers	5,000	5,000	5,000
6. Language Preparatory Courses/materials/ faculty & student stipends	5,000	38,000	38,000
7. LD Testing/Program Support for Adaptive Education	10,000	10,000	10,000
8. Writing Lab/Workshop/ CAI/hardware and software classes	10,000	5,000	5,000
9. PCUSA Seminary Consultation	0	20,000	0
10. Workshop at ATS Meeting	0	2,500	0
Yearly Totals	**60,000**	**131,655**	**110,446**
Grand Total:			**$302,101**

Budget Narrative

1. Personnel: The Director

The grant will pay 50% of the total share of the director's salary and benefits during the last two years of the granting period. The Seminary will pick up the other half during FY 2001 and FY 2002. It is the Seminary's intention to phase in this position as part of its academic affairs budget thereafter.

Work Study — Secretarial

The grant will pay for a quarter-time secretary to assist in the heavier start-up period of the program. It is the school's plan to switch secretarial support for the Director of Academic Support Services to the Student Affairs Secretary.

Writing Tutors

The employment of writing tutors will be initially supported by the grant but will be picked up as part of the academic affairs budget thereafter.

2. Moving and Search Expenses

We intend to limit our search to the regional area; therefore, we do not expect to pay for moving expenses.

3. Office Equipment for Two Offices

The offices in question are the Learning Center and the Director's Office. In addition to furniture for two adjacent conference rooms, the main work area, and the Director's area, facilities to accommodate a small library of resources should be available. The Director will also need a personal computer and printer, shelving space, and a small table with chairs for meeting purposes.

4. Orientation and Testing of First-Year Students

At a cost of $75 per student, we intend to conduct a full writing and language skills assessment of all entering first degree and international students during fall and spring orientation.

5. Faculty In-Service Training/Materials/Speakers

We plan six major seminars over three years, with calculated honoraria and travel expense of $750 per speaker, in addition to the cost of reading and learning material for twenty-five to thirty faculty and related staff members for each seminar.

6. Language Preparatory Course/Materials/Faculty/and Student Stipends

During the next two years, we want to conduct intensive language preparatory courses and offer students study stipends as replacement income for jobs they would otherwise take in order to come back to school the next term. The financial issue is a major barrier to participation, especially among racial/ethnic/minority students and older students with families. In addition, the grant would provide faculty stipends during the time-intensive development phase of the language preparatory program. The Seminary plans to raise endowment funds to support student language programs thereafter. Faculty stipends will be added to the academic affairs budget after the grant period expires in 2003.

7. LD Testing/Program Support for Adaptive Education

The Seminary will make arrangements to have students with undiagnosed learning disabilities tested at the School of Education of the University of Louisville. The cost per student is currently $400. In addition, there will be additional expenses related to consultations around each student's academic accommodation program.

8. Writing Center/Workshop/CAI/Hardware and Software/Classes

The Writing Center should contain six computers with Internet access and software for word processing. Additionally, the Seminary plans to install CAI software (Bible Tutor, for example) so that students can engage in self-paced, individualized learning. This budget line will also support the development of the *Writing Helps Program,* which will be open to all students.

9. PCUSA Consultation

Louisville Seminary will host a Presbyterian-wide consultation on academic support services in theological education. The cost of travel, housing, food, and meeting expenses for nine out-of-town delegations will be supported by the grant.

10. ATS Workshop

The grant would support two persons (travel, housing, related expenses) in their attendance at the ATS biennial meeting for purposes of conducting a workshop on academic readiness and strategies for addressing the teaching-learning needs of today's seminary students. The cost of the workshop materials is also anticipated in this budget line.

The finalized budget, whether one page or several, is now ready to include in the proposal document. Keep a copy of it with your backup worksheets in a special folder. The materials in this folder will assist you in tracking actual expenses as the project unfolds. They will enable you to anticipate lines that are in danger of going over budget or areas where you might have extra funds to spend, so that you can manage effectively the grant funds that you receive. These materials will also be extremely helpful when it comes time to write the grant report. An example of a program budget will be found in the sample proposal in Appendix A.

7

Developing the Master Proposal: Organization Information and Conclusion

Organization Information

Normally the resume of your nonprofit organization should come at the end of your proposal. Your natural inclination may be to put this information up front in the document, but it is usually better first to sell the need for your project and *then* your agency's ability to carry it out.

It is not necessary to overwhelm the reader with facts about your organization. This information can be conveyed easily by attaching a brochure or other prepared statement or by providing brief information and then referring the funder to your organization's Web site, if you have one. In two pages or less, tell the reader when your nonprofit came into existence; state its mission, being certain to demonstrate how the subject of the proposal fits within or extends that mission; and describe the organization's structure, programs, and special staff expertise. The following example is taken from WomenVenture's proposal.

Organization Overview

WomenVenture is a nationally recognized resource for women striving to find jobs, plan careers, and start and grow businesses. The agency has offered quality services to women in Minnesota with successful outcomes since 1978. By being future-focused, WomenVenture has been particularly successful in responding to state and federal welfare change, helping women who are making the transition off of welfare seek careers that will support their families. WomenVenture is a conduit to employers who will offer the agency's graduates jobs with livable wages, medical benefits, and ongoing training. In this way, WomenVenture accomplishes its mission to assist women in securing their own economic success and prosperity.

Since 1978, WomenVenture has helped more than 51,000 women and men of diverse ethnic, educational, and economic backgrounds move toward economic success. In 1999, based on information from those clients who provided data, 46 percent had household income of less than $20,000; 18 percent relied on public assistance; and 30 percent had no formal education beyond high school. Forty percent of clients providing data were people of color, illustrating WomenVenture's ability to reach a diverse community.

WomenVenture's three-year strategic plan has positioned the agency to make essential program shifts and to create new programs. The agency continuously works to improve, expand, and seek out opportunities to serve more customers, generate new sources of revenue, and sustain this organization. WomenVenture is committed to reaching low-income women and women throughout Minnesota who have multiple barriers, understanding their individual needs and working with them to identify and implement solutions. Through all of its programs and initiatives, WomenVenture transforms women's lives while strengthening families and communities.

Discuss the size of the board, how board members are recruited, and their level of participation. Give the reader a feel for the makeup of the board. (You should include the full board list in the appendix.) If your agency is composed of volunteers or has an active volunteer group, describe the functions that the volunteers fill. Provide details on the staff, including numbers of full- and part-time staff and their levels of expertise.

Describe the kinds of activities in which your staff engage. Explain briefly the assistance you provide. Describe the audiences you serve, any special or unusual needs they face, and why they rely on your agency. Cite the number of people who are reached through your programs.

Tying all of the information about your nonprofit together, cite your agency's expertise, especially as it relates to the subject of your proposal.

This information, coupled with the attachments you will supply in the appendix, is all the funder will require at this stage. Keep in mind that funders may wish to check with other sources to help evaluate your organization and its performance.

These sources might include experts in the field, contacts established at organizations similar to your own, other funders, or even an agency such as the BBB Wise Giving Alliance, which issues reports on some of the larger, national groups.

In the next sample, the Morristown Neighborhood House in a proposal to the Hyde and Watson Foundation briefly describes its history.

Brief History And Background

Founded in 1898, Neighborhood House was originally conceived by a small group of people who believed then that Italian immigrants would benefit from an agency that would assist them in becoming acclimated to a new culture and environment. In 1901, a building located on Flagler Street was donated to the founding committee to house the program. In 1923, incorporated as Morristown Neighborhood House, the Agency became a member of the Community Chest (which later became United Way). It was here at Neighborhood House that several local agencies first got their start, including the Urban

---

League of Morris County, the Visiting Nurse Association, the Colonial Little Symphony, and the New Jersey Chorale Society. Even the Morris Museum of Arts and Sciences, originally named "The Children's Museum," had its beginning in a room at Neighborhood House. The Neighborhood House has remained in the same location for 100 years. The organization has been helping to improve the quality of life for Morris County families for 102 years. During that time, the community experienced shifts in the ethnic make up of the community. Irish immigrants, African-Americans, and, most recently Hispanic-Latinos, who are becoming a growing segment of the Morristown community, have been the beneficiaries of programs offered at Neighborhood House.

Conclusion

Every proposal should have a concluding paragraph or two. This is a good place to call attention to the future, after the grant is completed. If appropriate, you should outline some of the follow-up activities that might be undertaken, to begin to prepare your funders for your next request.

This section is also the place to make a final appeal for your project. Briefly reiterate what your nonprofit wants to do and why it is important. Underscore why your agency needs funding to accomplish it. Don't be afraid at this stage to use a bit of emotion to solidify your case.

Two examples follow. The first is the conclusion to a proposal from the AIDS Resource Foundation for Children to the Hyde and Watson Foundation. It is a strong restatement of the facts that appeared in the body of the proposal.

Summary

The need for supportive services targeted to the at-risk population of children and adolescents coping with HIV/AIDS is enormous. With the establishment of the pediatric and teen health clinic and education center, the ARFC will meet the basic health care needs of infants, children, and adolescents who are infected/affected by HIV/AIDS. The educational services will use computer-assisted instruction and one-on-one tutoring to help the children and adolescents excel and receive a high school diploma. This program will be a collaborative effort with area hospitals, community health organizations, and local colleges and social service agencies.

The funding requested will support the renovations of the building. This project will provide a generation of at-risk youth with the opportunity to receive the health care and educational support needed to begin and maintain a higher quality of life. It will help them succeed despite the obstacles of growing up in a family devastated by AIDS.

The second example is from a proposal submitted by the Minnesota Opera to the General Mills Foundation. It is quite inspirational.

Conclusion

The Minnesota Opera is producing opera of a quality that rivals much of what can be seen around the world. We have internationally renowned artists at the top of their form, like Sumi Jo and Vivica Genaux. We have one of the most revered choruses in the world. We have worked hard to improve The Minnesota Opera orchestra over the last several years, and the ensemble makes substantial progress with every performance. Our artistic philosophy emphasizes the beautiful voice as central to our work, but rather than channel all our resources into a single component like star signers, we invest in every aspect of production. We believe that beautiful singing must be supported by all other operations, from the rehearsal process to the chorus and orchestra to the sets and costumes, and they must all be of a consistently high quality.

What local audiences get from The Minnesota Opera is great opera that is comparable to the work of opera companies across the globe. Our educational programming and outreach efforts ensure that people of diverse ages, cultures, and economic backgrounds from across the Upper Midwest are welcomed into the opera experience. Evaluation of these programs has been revised to provide more substantive information for everyone involved. We have a professional training program that has fostered nationally recognized talent, the likes of which only exists for companies more than two-three times our size. All of this stems from our passion to produce operas that are sung beautifully and presented with thoughtfulness and balance.

It is this commitment to artistry, and the continued generosity of our community, that will secure our success during this pivotal year of artistic expansion. Please support our fiscal 2001 efforts with a contribution of $40,000.

8

Variations on the Master Proposal Format

In the preceding chapters we presented the recommended format for components of the standard proposal. In reality, however, not every proposal will slavishly adhere to these guidelines. This should not be surprising. Sometimes the scale of the project might suggest a small-scale letter format proposal, or the type of request might not require all of the proposal components or the components in the sequence recommended here. The guidelines and policies of individual funders will be your ultimate guide. Many funders today state that they prefer a brief letter proposal; others require that you complete an application form. In any case, you will want to refer to the basic proposal components (see Chapter 2) to be sure that you have not omitted an element that will support your case.

What follows is a description of a letter proposal and of other format variations.

A Letter Proposal

The scale of the project will often determine whether it requires a letter or the longer proposal format. For example, a request to purchase a $1,000 fax machine for your agency simply does not lend itself to a lengthy narrative. A small contribution to your agency's annual operating budget, particularly if it is a renewal of past support, might also warrant a letter rather than a full-scale proposal.

What are the elements of a letter request? For the most part, they should follow the format of a full proposal, except with regard to length. The letter should be no more than three pages. You will need to call upon your writing skills because it can be very hard to get all of the necessary details into a concise, well-articulated letter.

As to the flow of information, follow these steps while keeping in mind that you are writing a letter to someone. It should not be as formal in style as a longer proposal would be. It may be necessary to change the sequence of the text to achieve the correct tone and the right flow of information.

Here are the components of a good letter proposal, with excerpts of relevant sections of a letter proposal from the Claremont Neighborhood Centers.

Ask for the gift: The letter should begin with a reference to your prior contact with the funder, if any. State why you are writing and how much funding is required from the particular foundation.

Dear _____:

Each year, Claremont Neighborhood Centers' Educational Learning Center (ELC) motivates youngsters to begin to take meaningful steps toward reaching their full potential. We know that to make a difference in the lives of the South Bronx youth ages 6–13 whom we serve each day, we must help them acquire both social and academic tools. To promote change and achievement, the ELC staff design creative activities that motivate children to learn.

In 1999–2000, Claremont continues to develop effective new program components, including a reading resource room, science activities, parent outreach, and improved communication with local schools. We have also recently added a new full-time Director of Educational Services to oversee and carry forward the growth and development of Claremont's Educational Learning Center.

It is our hope that _____ will work in partnership with Claremont to help us develop the Educational Learning Center. The support of _____ in the amount of $_____ will help us to continue to enhance and improve the Educational Learning Center.

Describe the need: In a very abbreviated manner, tell the funder why there is a need for this project, piece of equipment, etc.

Our Greatest Needs

Presently, our children's greatest educational needs are basic skills building in math and reading. The results of fourth-grade reading tests administered in 1999 showed over 80% of our young people needing significant extra help to perform at grade level. As the only community center in the immediate area, Claremont must assume a critical leadership role in providing our children with the opportunity to progress academically. Area Policy Board #3 has identified the school drop-out rate, illiteracy, and substance abuse as the three primary problems threatening our youngsters' academic progress.

Explain what you will do: Just as you would in a fuller proposal, provide enough detail to pique the funder's interest. Describe precisely what will take place as a result of the grant.

The Educational Learning Center

Claremont's Educational Learning Center focuses on the academic and personal development of our children, who hold the key to our neighborhood's future. The ELC fosters the academic and social skills that our children will need to grow up to become empowered and self-reliant adults.

Claremont hopes that through participation in the program our young people will gain:

- sound fundamental reading and math skills
- motivation to learn and an understanding of the importance of academic achievement
- new interests that inspire them to learn and expand their horizons
- healthy socialization and the development of friendships
- strong values and respect for others

New for 1999–2000

Claremont recognizes that communication between all parties involved in a child's education is also a vital element in academic achievement. Toward this end, our new full-time Director of Educational Services, Michel A. Williams, works with our parents to encourage open lines of communication between home, school, and the ELC. Mr. Williams is helping parents become more assured and effective advocates when dealing with schools (most of the children attend P. S. 132 and P. S. 55) and teachers. Mr. Williams has also recently organized and held the first meetings of our new Parent Advisory Committee.

In addition, we have implemented new Rules of Conduct (attached) for the children to follow. Also, we are starting a series of talks called Literacy Hour, where successful professionals from a variety of professions including the arts and Wall Street will meet with the children and help them to understand the importance of education in everyday life. Our newly refurbished and equipped computer room has allowed us to start a Computer Club for youngsters seeking more intensive instruction. We have also set aside an entire classroom (currently unoccupied) which we are transforming into a Reading Resource Library, where we can provide extra literacy assistance and also allow parents and children to read together.

Our Program

The Educational Learning Center presently serves from 80–100 children ages 6–13 each day. The Educational Learning Center's program hours run Monday through Friday from 2:15 p.m or 3:00 p.m (depending on the age group) to 6:00 p.m. The program day begins when escorts meet the children at their schools and walk with them to Claremont. Escorts are responsible for being at the school when children are dismissed, exercising control over the children as they walk to Claremont, and making sure that children are quiet and orderly before they enter the building. The discipline demanded of the children as they line up and travel to the Center prepares them for sustained positive behavior during their afternoon at the ELC. . . .

Many of the children living in our neighborhood also need to raise their self-esteem and to develop a sense of hope, in addition to enhancing their academic skills. The ELC fulfills this need through extracurricular activities designed to provide our children with cultural enrichment and encourage new interests that inspire them to learn and expand their horizons. Along with teaching valuable academic lessons, these activities encourage healthy socialization and development of strong values. . . .

These activities are chosen to empower children with the ability to perform at or above grade level as well as to develop interpersonal and creative skills, which are vitally important to the child's overall academic achievement. For outdoor recreational activities, there is a playground with a basketball court. Following the recreation period, the children conclude the day with a hot meal before their parents pick them up to go home.

Provide agency data: Help the funder know a bit more about your organization by including your mission statement, brief description of programs offered, number of people served, and staff, volunteer, and board data, if appropriate.

History And Purpose

Founded in 1956, Claremont Neighborhood Centers, Inc. is dedicated to improving the quality of life for residents of the Claremont/Morrisania area of the South Bronx. Claremont's mission is to provide programs and services that assist our constituency to build solid foundations that lead to personal and professional achievement and self-reliance. Claremont's major goals include decreasing the school drop-out rate of our youth through academic skill building and increasing family self-sufficiency through supportive services, such as day care, job readiness training, and adult continuing education.

Include appropriate budget data: Even a letter request may have a budget that is a half page long. Decide if this information should be incorporated into the letter or in a separate attachment. Whichever course you choose, be sure to indicate the total cost of the project. Discuss future funding only if the absence of this information will raise questions.

Close: As with the longer proposal, a letter proposal needs a strong concluding statement.

Conclusion

Claremont Neighborhood Centers has developed the Educational Learning Center to provide our children with a comprehensive program that meets their needs for basic skills education and helps them overcome the negative influences of their environment. In the coming year, our staff will continue to identify creative ways of motivating children to learn, creating and maintaining excitement for educational activities and encouraging parental responsibility and involvement in their children's academic progress. We hope that Claremont and

---

_____ will have the opportunity to work together on behalf of young people in the South Bronx.

I hope that you will call me at (718) 588-1000 x11 if you have any questions about our Educational Learning Center, or if you would like to arrange a visit to Claremont Neighborhood Centers.

Thank you for your consideration.

Sincerely,
Rachel E. Spivey
Executive Director

Attach any additional information required: The funder may need much of the same information to back up a small request as a large one: a board list, a copy of your IRS determination letter, financial documentation, and brief resumes of key staff. Rather than preparing a separate appendix, you should list the attachments at the end of a letter proposal, following the signature.

It may take as much thought and data gathering to write a good letter request as it does to prepare a full proposal (and sometimes even more). Don't assume that because it is only a letter, it isn't a time-consuming and challenging task. Every document you put in front of a funder says something about your agency. Each step you take with a funder should build a relationship for the future.

Other Variations in Format

Just as the scale of the project will dictate whether a letter or a full proposal is indicated, so the type of request will be the determining factor as to whether all of the components of a full proposal are required.

The following section will explore the information that should appear in the proposal application for five different types of requests: special project, general purpose, capital, endowment, and purchase of equipment.

Special Project

The basic proposal format presented in earlier chapters uses the special project proposal as the prototype, because this is the type of proposal that you will most often be required to design. As stated previously, funders tend to prefer to make grants for specific projects because such projects are finite and tangible, and their results are measurable. Most special project proposals will follow this format, or these basic components will be developed in a letter.

General Purpose

A general purpose proposal requests operating support for your agency. Therefore, it focuses more broadly on your organization, rather than on a specific project. All of the information in the standard proposal should be present, but there will not be a separate component describing your organization. That information will be the main thrust of the entire proposal. Also, your proposal budget will be the budget for the entire organization, so it need not be duplicated in the appendix.

Two components of the general purpose proposal deserve special attention. They are the need statement and program information, which replaces the "project description" component. The need section is especially important. You must make the case for your non-profit organization itself, and you must do it succinctly. What are the circumstances that led to the creation of your agency? Are those circumstances still urgent today? Use language that involves the reader, but be logical in the presentation of supporting data. For example, a local organization should cite local statistics, not national ones.

The following is an example of a need statement from a general purpose proposal for the Ronald McDonald House of New York.

Statement of Need

Cancer continues to be a leading disease and cause of death in children ages one to 14 in the United States. While increasingly sophisticated treatment strategies enable more children to win their battle against cancer and go on to lead normal, healthy lives, rare and severe forms of cancer continue to threaten the lives of too many children. A child's struggle against the disease is made even more difficult by the fact that model treatment programs are available only at a handful of hospitals in the United States, often far from home. Many of these model treatment

---

programs are located in New York City, such as Memorial Sloan-Kettering Cancer Center, The Mount Sinai Medical Center, and New York Hospital-Cornell Medical Center, all of which have been designated as "comprehensive cancer treatment centers" by the U.S. Department of Health and Human Services. Pediatric oncologists from across the country and around the world frequently advise families to seek treatment for their children at one of these renowned treatment centers.

Cancer therapy and its side effects are often frightening and painful, especially when the patient is a child. Furthermore, it can be difficult for children to remain positive and hopeful when facing cancer treatment alone, without the company and support of their loved ones. Maintaining familial bonds is critical to a child's emotional response to treatment, which can contribute greatly to a successful recovery. Research has shown that keeping children and their families together during cancer therapy alleviates physical and emotional stress, thus increasing the rate of successful treatment and recovery.

Parents also face a great deal of stress, both emotionally and financially, when their child undergoes cancer treatment. Although encouraged that their child is receiving the highest quality medical care in New York City, they are forced to passively observe their child endure a great deal of pain and trauma. Parents often feel a sense of isolation and helplessness as they must leave their homes and interrupt their lives for an extended period while dealing with a hospital environment that may be intimidating.

Furthermore, chemotherapy, hospitalization, and leave of absence from work place severe financial pressures on families, especially for those with modest incomes. The shift to managed care systems means that more parents are having to pay more out of their own pockets to bring their children to New York City medical centers. In addition, health care providers may specify a New York City medical center as the primary caregiver for a family from another region of the country, especially if the New York hospital's prices are more competitive. Many parents are more than willing to shoulder the extra financial burden if it means quality care, especially for the most difficult cases. However, handling this burden leaves little or no money for such necessities as travel, accommodations, and food, creating an acute crisis at a time when the parents' resources, both financial and emotional, are already stretched thin.

Consider including details on recent accomplishments and future directions as seen in this excerpt from the Ronald McDonald House proposal.

The Ronald McDonald House Today

Many exciting things have been going on at the Ronald McDonald House of New York. Over the past year, the House has worked to enhance our children's programming. Fun and enriching activities help maintain the children's education without interruption and introduce them to new skills and experiences. They also relieve stress, minimizing the negative impact of their treatment and ultimately building their self-esteem, a crucial element for recovery. We have made great strides with this initiative:

- *Homework Help* is offered five days per week.
- With both *Arts and Crafts* and *Self-Expression Art,* classes are offered three days per week.
- *One-on-One Music Lessons* are offered weekly, in which children can learn about music and a particular instrument, such as piano, drums, voice, or violin—recitals are organized each month for the children to demonstrate what they have learned.
- As a result of a generous grant from The Louis Calder Foundation, we now have a *Computer Lab,* which is open 24 hours per day.

In addition to these programs, the Ronald McDonald House continues to fill its calendar with fun activities: birthday parties, special dinners, magic shows, movies, Chess Club, Tai Chi, bingo, baking, outings to musicals, and trips to New York City cultural sites. We even have Scouting Troops for both boys and girls. We are constantly looking for new ways to help make life for our young patients more pleasant and uplifting. This task would be virtually impossible without the vital support provided by our compassionate staff, dedicated volunteers, and generous businesses from the community. Inner gifts of goodness and charity are what make the House so successful in serving the children and families.

Capital

A capital proposal requests funds for facility purchase, construction, or renovation, or possibly land purchase or long-term physical plant improvements. Today many institutions include other items in a capital campaign, such as endowment funds, program expansion, and salaries for professors. But, for our purposes, we will discuss the more traditional definition of capital, that is, "bricks and mortar."

All of the components of a proposal will be included in a capital request. Differences in content will mainly be in the need statement, the project description, the budget, and the appendix.

The need section in the capital proposal should focus on why the construction or renovation is required. The challenge is to make the programs that will use the facility come alive to the reader. For example, your agency may need to expand its day care program because of the tremendous need in your community among working parents for such support, the long waiting list you have, and the potential educational value to the children. Your proposal will be less compelling if the focus of the need statement is purely related to space considerations or to meeting building code requirements.

Following is an excerpt from a capital proposal for The Children's Institute.

The Need

Our children come to us having experienced frustration and failure within their local school districts. It is our job, based on their potential, to return them to their local school district and to prepare them for a productive life in society. They have special requirements, which dictate the design of a physical setting for them. It is important to point out that TCI has served children successfully in less than adequate physical surroundings. Imagine what we will be able to accomplish in an enlarged setting and an appropriately designed space!

A lack of space has inhibited our ability to expand the scope of our programs and services.

What are our children's needs?

1. Each child has a different set of social, emotional, educational, and physical problems. For the child to succeed, it is

essential that the teacher provide the individual attention and support required. Students' learning problems are addressed in prescriptive individualized education plans that are carefully developed for each student. In order to adequately meet the unique needs of the students, TCI provides a high staff-to-student ratio. Hence, more classrooms are needed for fewer children. And classroom space must be flexible to allow for numerous learning activities to occur at one time.

2. Students require a model alternative program that will nurture their self-esteem and increase their ability to resolve problems and express feelings in a positive way. TCI provides children with a wide array of therapeutic services, including individual, group, and family counseling and psychiatric and psychological consultation.

   A nationally recognized social problem-solving and social skill curriculum has been implemented school wide, based on the premise that children can avoid self-destructive behavior and succeed later in life if they learn while they are young how to get along with others and cope with problems. Problem-solving areas, counseling rooms, and offices will be provided throughout the building to ensure adequate therapeutic services and supports.

3. The children need special auxiliary programs, which in turn translate into special space. A few examples follow:

   a. To develop gross and fine motor skills and enhance sensory integration, areas are needed for adaptive physical activity. Hence, a gym and multi-sensory room and areas for occupational and physical therapy are critical.

   b. To meet the needs of different learning abilities, a well equipped multi-media center and computer technology laboratory are essential.

   c. Many older youth will move directly from their educational experience to independent living and jobs. It is TCI's obligation to help them develop life skills. Specially designed spaces to replicate work and living spaces are required.

A special school of their own will mean that our children will, for the first time, have space designed to meet their unique needs.

The project description component of a capital proposal includes two elements. The first is the description of how your programs will be enhanced or altered as a result of the physical work. Then should come a description of the physical work itself. The funder is being asked to pay for the latter and should have a complete narrative on the work to be undertaken. You might supplement that description with drawings, if available. These could be external views of the facility, as well as interior sketches showing people using the facility. Floor plans might help as well. These need not be formal renderings by an artist or an architect; a well-drawn diagram will often make the case. Photos showing "before" and drawings indicating what the "after" will be like are also dramatic adjuncts to the capital proposal.

The budget for a capital proposal will be a very detailed delineation of all costs related to the construction, renovation, etc. It should include the following:

- actual brick and mortar expenses. These should be presented in some logical sequence related to the work being undertaken. For example, a renovation project might follow an area-by-area description, or a construction project might be presented chronologically. Don't forget to include expenses for such items as construction permits in this section.

- other costs: salaries, fees, and related expenses required to undertake the capital improvements. Be certain to include in your budget the projected costs of architects, lawyers, and public relations and fundraising professionals. Many capital proposal writers fail to adequately anticipate such "soft" costs.

- contingency: Estimates for actual construction costs often change during the fundraising and preconstruction periods. It is therefore a good idea to build a contingency into the budget in case costs exceed the budgeted amounts. A contingency of 10 to 20 percent is the norm; more than that tends to raise a proposal reviewer's eyebrows.

Here is the capital campaign budget for The Children's Institute.

Projected Capital Campaign Budget	
Construction/Renovation	$3,962,700
Equipment	$ 175,000
Furnishings	$ 125,000
Fees	$ 350,000
Contingency	$ 396,270
Fundraising Expense	$ 100,000
Interest Expense	$ 67,500
Other:	
Clerk of the Works	$ 30,000
Elevator Renovation	$ 45,000
Other:	
Computer Tech Wiring	$ 80,000
Bond Origination Costs	$ 100,000
Asbestos Removal	$ 440,000
Project Cost—Site Work	$ 200,000
Total Costs	**$6,071,470**

The appendix to a capital proposal may be expanded to include floor plans and renderings if they do not appear within the proposal text. If a brochure has been developed in conjunction with the capital campaign, this could be sent along as part of the appendix package.

Endowment

An endowment is used by nonprofits to provide financial stability and to supplement grant and earned income. Often campaigns, designed like capital drives, are mounted to attract endowment dollars. A proposal specifically requesting funding for endowment may resemble either a special project or a general operating application, depending on whether the endowment is for a special purpose, such as scholarships or faculty salaries, or for the organization's general operations. Your focus will be on the following components: the need statement, the program description, and the budget.

The need statement for an endowment proposal will highlight why the organization must establish or add to its endowment. Points to raise might include:

- the importance of having available the interest from the endowment's corpus as an adjunct to the operating budget;
- the desire to stabilize annual income, which is currently subject to the vagaries of government or other grants;
- the value of endowing a particular activity of your organization that lacks the capacity to earn income or attract gift support.

The project description will cover the impact of endowment dollars on the programs of your nonprofit. Provide as many details as possible in explaining the direct consequences of these dollars. Indicate if there are naming or memorial opportunities as part of the endowment fund.

The budget will round out all of this data by indicating how much you are trying to raise and in what categories. For example, there might be a need to endow 75 scholarships at $10,000 each for a total of $750,000.

Equipment

Frequently, organizations have a need to develop a free-standing proposal for purchase of a piece of equipment, be it MRI equipment for a hospital or a personal computer for program staff. These would require only a letter proposal, but the scale or significance of the purchase may dictate a full proposal. Again, the need statement, the project description, and the budget will be primary.

In the need statement, explain why the organization must have this equipment. For example, this hospital has no MRI equipment, and people in the community have to travel great distances when an MRI test is required.

Then in the project description, explain how the equipment will alter the way services are delivered. For example: "The new MRI equipment will serve some 500 people annually. It will assist in diagnoses ranging from structural problems in the foot to tracking the development of a lung tumor. The cost per procedure will be $1,000, but it will save millions in unnecessary surgical procedures."

This budget may be the easiest you will ever have to prepare. Indicate the purchase cost for the equipment, plus transportation and installation charges. Consider whether staff training to utilize the equipment properly and the added expenses of maintenance contracts should be included in your budget with the cost of its purchase.

9

Packaging the Proposal

Writing a well-articulated proposal represents the bulk of the effort in preparing a solid proposal package. The remaining work is to package the document for the particular funder to whom it is being sent, based on your research and your contact with that funder to date (as described in Chapters 10 and 11).

Be sure to check the foundation's instructions for how and when to apply. Some foundations will accept proposals at any time. Others have specific deadlines. Foundations will also differ in the materials they want a grant applicant to submit. Some will list the specific information they want and the format you should adopt. Others will have an application form. In the course of the interviews for this book, it became apparent that an increasing number of foundations are developing an application form or a specific proposal format as a means of helping staff look at diverse information in a concise and consistent manner. Many are posting these guidelines on their Web sites. Whatever the foundation's guidelines, pay careful attention to them and follow them.

Jonathan Howe of the Arthur Vining Davis Foundations makes this point: "If your project doesn't fit, it is a waste of postage to apply. So many requests are clearly not within our guidelines."

In the following pages we will discuss the packaging of the document, including:

- cover letter or letter of transmittal;
- cover and title pages;
- table of contents; and
- appendix.

The Cover Letter

Often the cover letter is the basis for either consideration or rejection. Hildy Simmons of J. P. Morgan Charitable Trust states, "The cover letter is key. It should be clear and concise and make me want to turn the page. Here are a few dos and don'ts:

- Do make a specific request. It's inconvenient if we have to dig for it.
- Do include a couple of paragraphs about why you are applying to us. But don't quote back to us our own contribution report.
- Do note references but don't name drop."

Julie Rogers of the Eugene and Agnes E. Meyer Foundation advises, "The cover letter is the best shot to make the proposal compelling. It should be humanizing."

What a waste of your agency's resources to invest time, energy, and money developing a proposal around a terrific project and then not have it read! To avoid this happening, be clear, be succinct, and state immediately why the project fits within the funder's guidelines. For example, you might state, "Our funding research indicates that the XYZ Foundation has a special interest in the needs of children in foster care, which is the focus of this proposal." If the proposal does not fit the foundation's guidelines, this should be acknowledged immediately in the cover letter. You will then need to provide an explanation for why you are approaching this foundation.

If you had a conversation with someone in the funder's office prior to submitting the proposal, the cover letter should refer to it. For example, you might say, "I appreciate the time Jane Doe of your staff took to speak with me on December 1 about the Foundation." But do *not* imply that a proposal was requested if in fact it was not.

Sometimes in a discussion with a funder you will be told, "I can't encourage you to submit because. . . . However, if you want, you can go ahead and submit anyway." In this case, you should still refer to the conversation, but your letter should demonstrate that you heard what the funder said. Andrew Lark of the Frances L. & Edwin L. Cummings Memorial Fund encourages grantseekers to call *after* they have carefully read the Fund's guidelines, but he wants subsequent correspondence to accurately reflect that conversation: "If we have had past contact or if we have ever funded you, remind us of that. But be careful how the letter reflects a prior conversation—avoid exaggeration."

The cover letter should also indicate what the reader will find in the proposal package. For example: "You will find enclosed two documents for your review. The first is a concise description of our project. The second is an appendix with the documents required by the Foundation for further review of our request."

Cite the name of the project, a precis of what it will accomplish, and the dollar amount of the request. For example: "Our After School Recreational Program will meet the educational and recreational needs of 50 disadvantaged Harlem children. We are seeking a grant of $25,000 from the Foundation to launch this project."

In the concluding paragraph of the cover letter, you should request a meeting with the funder. This can take place at the funder's office or on site at your agency. Also indicate your willingness to answer any questions that might arise or to provide additional information as required by the funder.

In summary, the cover letter should:

- indicate the size of the request;
- state why you are approaching this funder;
- mention any prior discussion of the proposal;
- describe the contents of the proposal package;

- briefly explain the project; and
- offer to set up a meeting and to provide additional information.

Who should sign the letter? Either the chairman of the board or the chief executive officer of your agency should be the spokesperson for all proposal submissions. Some funders insist on signature by the chairman of the board, indicating that the proposal has the support and endorsement of the board. However, signature by the executive director may allow for a sense of continuity that a rotating board chair cannot provide. If your group has no full-time staff, then the issue is resolved for you, and the board chairman should sign all requests. This would hold true also if your agency is in the process of searching for a new chief executive.

The proposal cover letter should never be signed by a member of the development staff. These individuals do the research, develop the proposals, and communicate with the funder, but generally they stay in the background when it comes to the submission of the proposal and any meetings with the funder. The individual who signs the cover letter should be the same person who signs subsequent correspondence, so that the organization has one spokesperson.

Variations may occur under special circumstances. For example, if a board member other than the chairperson is directly soliciting a peer, the cover letter should come from him or her. Alternatives would be for the letter to be signed by the chairman of the board and then for the board member to write a personal note on the original letter, or to send along a separate letter endorsing the proposal.

Following is a cover letter to the General Mills Foundation from WomenVenture. Note that the letter includes:

- reference to prior support;
- the request;
- information about the project and the organization;
- some examples; and
- a promise to supply additional information, if needed.

Reatha Clark King, Ph.D.
President and Executive Director
General Mills Foundation
Post Office Box 1113
Minneapolis, MN 55440

Dear Dr. King:

Thank you again for the enormously generous support you and the General Mills Foundation provided to Women-Venture in 1999. Last year, WomenVenture helped 3,154 clients achieve economic success and prosperity, which is Women-Venture's mission. We are requesting a total grant of $40,000 from the General Mills Foundation—$20,000 to support WomenVenture's services and strategies and $20,000 to support the WomenVenture's family-focused Intergenerational Program.

In this era of prosperity, it is possible to lose sight of the fact that low-income women are struggling to overcome significant barriers to their success. WomenVenture remains committed to assisting low-income women in overcoming those barriers and breaking the cycle of poverty.

WomenVenture accomplishes its mission by providing training, education, and support to people who want to find jobs with livable wages, change or develop a career, or start or expand a business. As clients develop career and employment options, they also gain the skills they need to successfully manage their personal finances.

The General Mills Foundation's interest in youth and family life aligns closely with our innovative Intergenerational Program. The Intergenerational Program provides early intervention for welfare-dependent girls, ages nine to thirteen, and for their mothers. The program establishes a support system that strengthens the family as a whole while mothers make their transition into the workforce. Girls enrolled in the program receive early career training and begin to develop individual life plans. The girls continue to receive support from the program until their high school graduation. This program is predicated on the importance of the interrelationships among daughters and mothers, their families and communities, and the role these relationships play in the eventual success of breaking generational cycles of poverty.

We are currently engaged in discussions that will allow us to expand our services into Minneapolis' north side communities. Building on our experience of offering services at the Sabathani Community Center in Minneapolis and St. Paul's Frogtown Action Alliance, we are looking at similar collaborations with Pillsbury Neighborhood Services, the Minneapolis Urban League, and Summit Academy OIC.

WomenVeture needs your help. In partnership with the General Mills Foundation, we will continue to address the needs of our clients so that they can become economically successful. In this way, our clients become role models for their families, for their communities, and for other women who still struggle.

Please let me know if there is additional information that will help you make a decision to fund WomenVenture's work and mission. Thank you so much for your support and for your consideration.

Sincerely,

Tené Heidelberg
President of WomenVenture

Here is another example of a cover letter, this one from The Field. It has the following characteristics:

- It is very brief.
- It requests specific support.
- It describes past successes and future plans.

Edward L. Jones, Vice President
Morgan Guaranty Trust Company of New York
60 Wall Street, 46th Floor
New York, NY 10260-0060

Dear Mr. Jones:

Enclosed is The Field's request for a grant in the amount of $10,000 to support our programs that serve performing artists and their audiences in New York City. This year, we plan to build on our partnerships with organizations city wide to give artists who may not already know about us the chance to participate in our programs.

1998 proved to be exciting and impactful for The Field:

- The number of independent artists and companies joining The Field as members doubled;
- Artists using our Career-Based programs, Group, Pairs, and Consulting, doubled;
- The funds raised on behalf of Field members increased by 82%, reaching $354,000;
- As part of our continuing marketing and outreach effort, we established two new organizational partnerships with Dancing in the Streets and Dance Theater Workshop and designed and built our website, www.thefield.org.

We have developed two new programs for 1999, both of which help artists at various levels of their careers address a broad spectrum of concerns. *Artward Bound,* The Field's free, out-of-town residency program for performing artists, combines individual studio time for each participant with group workshops on creative and career issues. Initiated last year, *The Real Story* is an oral history and workshop program illustrating the myriad strategies artists use to sustain a life in the arts.

Enclosed, please find a project proposal and financial statements to complete our request for support from Morgan Guaranty Trust Company. If you have any questions or need further information, please don't hesitate to call me.

Best wishes,
Aaron Landsman
Development Director

A final example is from the YWCA of Plainfield/North Plainfield, New Jersey. It was well received by the grantmaker who was familiar with the applying organization. Sometimes candor—mixed with a touch of humor—can be very effective.

Mr. Robert Parsons, Jr.
Chairman
Charles E. & Joy C. Pettinos Foundation
437 Southern Boulevard
Chatham Township, NJ 07928

Dear Mr. Parsons:

I know, I know that my proposal is being submitted to you after March 1st. This is completely my fault, and I will understand if the foundation's managers determine that our request is ineligible for consideration at this time.

We have just entered into a new phase of the Campaign, and I have taken on a number of new responsibilities—and one of them was to submit this proposal. But I just didn't get up to speed in time.

If you are able to consider support for the YWCA, we will all be grateful. This is a big project for us, but it is going very well and we have experienced such kindness and generosity from so many in the past year.

Mr. Parsons, I appreciate your past support. If you are not able to accept this proposal now, I hope I will have the opportunity to resubmit at another time. But please don't report me to my Board!

Thank you again.

Sincerely,

Jacquelyn M. Glock, MSW
Executive Director

Cover Page and Title

The cover page has three functions:

1. to convey specific information to the reader;
2. to protect the proposal; and
3. to reflect the professionalism of the preparer.

You should personalize the information on the cover page by including the name of the funder. You might present the information as follows:

A PROPOSAL TO THE XYZ FOUNDATION

or

A REQUEST DEVELOPED FOR THE XYZ FOUNDATION

Then note the title of the project:

A CAMPAIGN FOR STABILITY

Provide key information that the funder might need to contact your agency:

Submitted by:
Mary Smith
Executive Director
The Nonprofit Organization
40 Canal Street
New York, NY 10013
212-935-5300

It is possible that your cover letter will be separated from the rest of the proposal. Without key information on the cover page, the funder could fail to follow up with your agency.

The cover page from the Alternatives for Community & Environment proposal serves as an example.

Alternatives for Community & Environment

Organizing and Capacity Building for Healthy, Livable, and Environmentally Just Communities in Greater Boston

Submitted to:
Hyams Foundation
Elizabeth B. Smith
Executive Director
175 Federal Street, 14th Floor
Boston, MA 02110

Submitted by:
Alternatives for Community & Environment, Inc.
Warren Goldstein-Gelb
Research & Development Director
2343 Washington Street, 2nd Floor
Roxbury, MA 02119
(617) 442-3343 x31

The title you assign to your proposal can have a surprisingly significant impact on the reader. It should reflect what your project is all about. "A CAMPAIGN FOR STABILITY" tells the reader that there is a formal effort taking place and that the result will be to bring stability to the nonprofit applicant. It is short and to the point, while being descriptive.

There are a few suggestions for developing the title for a proposal:

- Don't try to be cute. Fundraising is a serious matter. A cute title implies that the proposal is not a serious attempt to solve a real problem.

- Do not duplicate the title of another project in your agency or one of another nonprofit that might be well known to the funder. It can cause confusion.

- Be sure the title means something. If it is just words, try again, or don't use any title at all.

Coming up with the title can be a tricky part of proposal writing. If you are stuck, try these suggestions:

- Seek the advice of the executive director, the project director, or a creative person in the organization or outside.

- Hold an informal competition among staff and/or volunteers to see who can come up with the best title.

- Go to the board with a few ideas and ask board members to select the one that makes the most sense.

- Jot down a list of key words from the proposal. Add a verb or two and experiment with the word order.

Let's take a look at a few actual titles and evaluate their effectiveness.

Title	Effectiveness
Forward Face	Arouses interest but does not tell you anything about the project.
	This is a proposal that seeks funds for facial reconstruction for disfigured children. With the help of the nonprofit group involved, the children will have a new image with which to face the future. The title is a pun, which is cute but not very effective.
Vocational, Educational Employment Project	This title tells us that three types of services will be offered.
	The project serves disadvantaged youth, which is not mentioned. The effectiveness of this title could be improved if the population served were somehow alluded to.

Title	Effectiveness
Building a Healthier Tomorrow	This title implies that construction will occur, and indeed it is the title for a capital campaign. It also suggests that the construction is for some kind of health facility. This proposal is for a YMCA to improve its health-wellness facilities. Thus, the title is very effective in conveying the purpose of the proposal.

You should evaluate any titles you come up with by anticipating the reaction of the uninitiated funding representative who will be reading this proposal.

Table of Contents

Obviously, for letter proposals or those of five pages or less, a table of contents is not required. For proposals of ten pages or more, it is probably a very good idea to include it.

Simply put, the table of contents tells the reader what information will be found in the proposal. The various sections should be listed in the order in which they appear, with page numbers indicating where in the document they can be located. The table should be laid out in such a way that it takes up one full page.

Following the proposal format we have recommended, a table of contents would look like this:

TABLE OF CONTENTS	Page
Executive Summary	1
Statement of Need	2
Project Description	4
Budget	7
Organization Information	9
Conclusion	10

By stating where to find specific pieces of information, you are being considerate of the proposal reader, who might want an overview of what information is included and also might want to be selective in the initial review.

A sample follows. It is from a proposal for Heads Up.

Table of Contents

I. Narrative
    Organizational Background 1
    Purpose of Request: Goals and Objectives 3
    Organizational Capacity 5
    Process 5
    Evaluation Plan 9
    Sustainability 10
II. Finances
III. Attachments
    • IRS 501(c)(3) Letter of Determination
    • Key Staff Profiles
    • Board of Directors
    • Letters of Support
    • FY 1998 Audited Financial Statements
    • Additional Promotional Materials

The Appendix

The appendix is a reference tool for the funder. Include in it any information not included elsewhere that the foundation or corporate grantmaker indicates is required for review of your request. Not every proposal requires an appendix.

The appendix should be stapled together separately from the proposal narrative. Because it usually contains information that the funder has specifically requested, keeping it separate makes it easy for the funder to find those items. The appendix may have its own table of contents indicating to the reader what follows and where to find it.

A sample table of contents to a proposal appendix, taken from the Detroit Zoological Society proposal, follows:

Detroit Zoological Society

Proposal Attachments

1. Current Annual Operating Budget

2. Listing of Board of Directors

3. Letters of Cooperation/Support

4. Performance Analysis Chart

5. Annual Report for Members

6. Capital Project Descriptions
   • National Amphibian Conservation Center
   • Arctic Ring of Life
   • Conservation Education Center
   • Animal Health Complex

7. Tax-exempt Status Verification Letter

8. Audited Financial Statements

You may wish to include any or all of the following items in the appendix:

1. A board list. This should contain the name of each board member and that person's business or other affiliation. Adding further contact information such as address and telephone number is optional. The reader will use this to identify people he or she knows or whose names are familiar.

   An excerpt from the board list for Jobs for Youth-Boston, Inc. serves as an example:

Jobs for Youth
Board of Directors

Kevin F. Smith (Chair)
Director
Boston Bay Consulting

Otis A. Gates (Treasurer)
Chief Financial Officer
Long Bay Management Co.

Joseph C. Maher, Jr.
  (Secretary)
Partner
Foley, Hoag & Eliot

Alton L. Adams
CEO
PRG, Inc.

Sarah Allen
Vice President
Mellon New England

John W. Calkins
Consultant

Charles J. Clark
Senior Vice President
Citizens Bank

Walter R. Jennings
Consultant

Alicia Knoff
Evaluation Team Leader
William H. Taft Middle School

Kevin J. MacDonald
Partner
Mullen & Company, LLP

Daniel J. Sullivan, Jr.
President and CEO
Holographic Lithography
  Systems, Inc.

John L. Sullivan
Research Analyst and Vice
  President
Stephens, Inc.

Reginald H. White
Vice President
Fidelity Investments

Rogelio A. Whittington
President and CEO
Contacto, Inc.

---

2. Your nonprofit's IRS Letter of Determination. This document, issued by the IRS, indicates that your agency has been granted 501(c)(3) status and is "not a private foundation." Gifts made to your organization are deductible for tax purposes. This letter is usually requested by funders. Foundations can give most easily to publicly supported organizations, and corporations want their gifts to be tax deductible. If

your organization is religiously affiliated or a government entity, you might not have such a letter, and you should explain that fact to the funder.

3. Financial information. The operating budget for the current fiscal year and the latest audited financial statement are often appropriate to include. Some funders request your latest 990 in order to assess the financial stability of your organization. If your agency is religiously affiliated, or for some other reason you do not file a 990, you will need to explain this fact to a funder that requests it. You may want to include a list of donors for the past fiscal year by name and size of gift. Grantmakers also want to know which foundations and corporations currently are being approached to help with the project under review. Add that information, as well. An excerpt from the Operation Exodus Inner City, Inc. support list follows.

OPERATION EXODUS INNER CITY, INC.
List of Supporters

Funding Sources	1997–1998	1998–1999	1999–2000	2000–2001
American Chai Foundation			$2,000	
Anonymous Donors	$41,300	$60,000	$89,000	
Louis Calder Foundation			$15,000	$20,000
Chase Manhattan Foundation	$500	$1,000		
Con Edison			$500	
Cowen Foundation	$1,000			
Fortis Foundation		$500		
Lily Palmer Fry Foundation			$1,000	
Greentree Foundation	$5,000	$5,000		$5,000
Hope for New York	$6,500	$11,600	$15,000	
International Jewelers Underwriters	$1,250		$2,500	
J.P. Morgan	$1,000			
Kenworthy-Swift Foundation			$10,000	
Emily Davie & Joseph S. Kornfeld Foundation	$16,100	$37,150	$25,000	
Marsicano Foundation			$750	
Metzger-Price Fund, Inc.	$1,000	$1,000	$1,000	
Pincus Family Fund		$10,000		
Pinkerton Foundation		$15,000	$15,000	
Louis & Harold Price Foundation		$5,000		
Starr Foundation		$20,000	$30,000	
Sumitomo Corporation	$500			
Total	**$74,150**	**$166,250**	**$206,750**	**$25,000**

*Note: OEIC's fiscal year begins September 1 and ends August 31.

4. Resumes of key staff. If the background information on key staff members is not included as part of the project statement of the proposal, it should be included in the appendix. This also might be the place to include the organization chart, if you feel it would be helpful.

Do not include in the appendix anything that is not required by the funder or deemed essential to making your case. The key is to give the funder what is needed for review of your proposal without making the package look overwhelming. For example, many nonprofits like to add press clippings to the appendix. If they make the package appear unnecessarily bulky and are tangential to the grant review, they should be sent to the funder at another time when they will receive more attention. However, should these clippings be essential to the review of the request, then by all means include them.

At this stage of assembling the proposal, you have a cover letter and two additional separately packaged components: the proposal narrative and the appendix. If each is clearly identifiable, you will save the funder time and energy in the initial review of your proposal.

Packaging

Packaging refers to both the physical preparation of the documents and their assembly.

Physical Preparation

Every proposal package should be individually prepared for each funder. This permits you to customize the submission in order to reflect the interests of a specific funder and to show them that you've done your homework. This is the point at which you need to double-check the guidelines for a funder's specific requirements for the proposal package.

With today's word-processing software, it will be relatively easy to customize the cover letter, title page, and other components of the package that have variables in them. For those components that are photocopied, be sure that the originals you are working from are crisp and legible. For example, if your IRS Letter of Determination is in poor condition, write to the Internal Revenue Service at I.R.S.,

TE/GE, Room 4010, P.O. Box 2508, Cincinnati, OH 45201 (or call toll-free 1-877-829-5500), and ask for a fresh copy of the letter. The request must be on your organization's official letterhead. The letter should contain your organization's name, address, taxpayer ID number, and a daytime telephone number, and it must be signed by an officer with that person's title. For the other documents, copy from originals whenever possible.

Assembly

When a proposal arrives in a funder's office, any binding is usually removed before the proposal is reviewed. Therefore, do not waste money on binding for the proposal and the appendix. Simply staple each document, or use a plastic strip to hold together each document. Lynn Pattillo of the Pittulloch Foundation, Inc., says, "We prefer not to get big, glossy packages. If you spend too much on the package, you are taking away from your program."

You have three documents: the cover letter, the proposal, and the appendix. The latter two are separately stapled. In all likelihood, these documents will require a manila envelope. Be certain that the addressee and return address information are printed clearly on the envelope. You might want to put a piece of cardboard in the envelope to protect the documents. Then insert the three documents with the cover letter on top, followed by the proposal and the appendix.

With regard to the funder's address, if you are following the procedure recommended in Chapter 11 for submitting this request, you will have had a conversation with the funder's office prior to submitting the proposal. Use that opportunity to verify the address and the name of the person to whom the package is to be sent.

Of course, the prior advice assumes you will be mailing in a proposal to a funder via the U.S. Postal Service. A few of the grantmakers interviewed for this book indicate that they now accept proposals as documents attached to e-mail cover letters. Others say they expect to do so in the very near future. Still others are considering online application forms that grantseekers fill out and submit electronically. As John Murphy of the Flinn Foundation says, "Many foundations are working toward a more paper-free process." In many instances, however, the attachments such as the IRS designation letter, audited financials, and the organization's Form 990 still need to be mailed separately.

10

Researching Potential Funders

Once you have drafted your proposal, you are ready to develop your prospect list of foundations and/or corporations that might be interested in funding it. What you learn during this process will help you prepare different proposal packages, as described in Chapter 9, depending on the specific funder information you uncover.

The foundation and corporate executives interviewed for this book repeatedly advised grantseekers to pay special attention to the research effort. Most felt that sufficient information is available to enable nonprofit organizations to do their homework, thereby obtaining a clear picture of the interests of potential funders. As Hildy Simmons of J.P. Morgan Charitable Trust says, "Do your homework. This increases your chances to get funding. There is no quick fix or right contact, and no substitute for doing the work." David Odahowski of the Edyth Bush Charitable Foundation adds, "There is no magic bullet. You have to go through the process."

There are three steps you should follow in your research:

- Compile;
- Investigate;
- Refine.

Compile

Compile a list of foundations, corporations, and other funders whose geographic and/or program interests might lead them to support your agency and the specific projects for which you are seeking funding. Try to be inclusive at this stage. If you think a specific foundation or corporate donor should be on the list, go ahead and include it. Let further research on the source tell you otherwise.

At the compilation stage, you have a variety of resources to draw upon in addition to the standard print or online funding directories. Check your local newspaper for articles about corporations or businesses in your area. Talk to your local chamber of commerce and civic groups such as the Rotary and Lions Club. Utilize various search engines on the Internet. Be resourceful as you compile your list of possible funders.

You will also want to be aware of who is funding other agencies in your community. These foundations and corporations may be likely sources of support for your own agency. This information can be difficult to unearth. Sometimes another local agency's annual report or Web site will list its funders; nonprofits occasionally will publicly thank their funders in the local newspaper; arts organizations usually will list their donors in event programs. The grants database in *FC Search: The Foundation Center's Database on CD-ROM, The Foundation Directory Online Plus* and *Premium,* and the Foundation Center's *The Foundation Grants Index* in print and on CD-ROM contain the names of recipients of grants of $10,000 and up from 1,000 of the largest foundations.

Investigate

Next, take your list and investigate each source. There are definitive resources available to you to research foundations. The IRS requires foundations to file an annual 990-PF form reporting on assets and grants. You will base your research on directories that have been compiled using the 990-PF or from information provided directly to the directory publisher, on materials issued by the foundations themselves or on the 990-PF itself. It is more difficult to obtain information on corporate giving. As noted elsewhere, corporations may use two grantmaking vehicles: a private foundation and a corporate giving program. If a corporation has a foundation, then a 990-PF will be filed, just as with other private foundations. If the corporation has a separate giving program, it is not required to file a publicly available report on gifts made under this program. Some corporations do issue special reports on their philanthropic endeavors, and a number of directories devoted specifically to corporate giving are published regularly. Corporate Web sites can also yield useful information on company philanthropic endeavors, if you know where to look.

Here is what you are looking for in any of the resources you use:

- A track record of giving in your geographic locale, in your field of interest, or for the type of support you seek, be it basic operating support or funding for construction or equipment.
- Grants of a size compatible with your agency's needs. (Bear in mind that in all likelihood your project will have more than one funder.)
- Funders that have not already committed their resources many years into the future and that do not appear simply to fund the same nonprofit groups year in and year out.

Print and Electronic Directories

Appendix C contains a description of print and electronic resources you can utilize in your research. The Foundation Center is the preeminent source of information on foundation and corporate funders. *FC Search: The Foundation Center's Database on CD-ROM*, the Center's print directories, and many other resources are made available to the public at its libraries and Cooperating Collections in sites across the country. The Center's collections also include copies of foundation guidelines, annual reports, press releases, historical materials, and even newspaper clippings on local or national foundations. Where detailed database or annual report information is lacking, you can examine copies of a foundation's 990-PF at one of the Foundation Center's library collections or via Foundation Finder or the Private Foundation Tax Return Search at the Center's Web site (www.fdncenter.org). In addition, the Center's Web site offers *The Foundation Directory Online*, a family of searchable databases, available in a range of monthly subscription options.

Print and CD-ROM directories will most likely be your primary resource in investigating the foundations on your list. But you must not stop there. Often you will find additional or more up-to-date information in other resources, such as online subscription services and various Web sites.

The Internet

Grantseekers are discovering a wealth of information on the Internet. Although locating that information can be daunting at first, there are many helpful resources on the subject. The Foundation Center maintains its own content-rich Web site on the Internet. The Center's site is an easy-to-use gateway to a wide range of philanthropic information resources. Visitors to the site can readily access many other Internet sites, including those maintained by private, corporate, and community foundations; nonprofit organizations; government agencies; and other groups that provide information of interest to nonprofit organizations. For more in-depth information on mining the many Internet resources for grantseekers, see *The Foundation Center's Guide to Grantseeking on the Web*. This guide identifies useful sites for grantseekers and provides the "how-tos" of connecting to and effectively using the Internet for funding research.

At the Foundation Center's home page you will find a link to the "Search Zone." The Search Zone provides access to all search mechanisms at the Center's Web site from one central location, along with recommendations for the best search to conduct to find the information you seek. Also at our Web site you will find *Philanthropy News Digest (PND)*, our weekly online news abstracting service of philanthropy-related articles. Besides keeping grantseekers and others abreast of recent and significant developments in the world of philanthropy, *PND* also includes weekly Web site and/or book reviews, a spotlight on various nonprofit organizations, an RFP Bulletin, a job corner, a conference calendar, and more.

The information on the Internet, and the tools used to search it, are constantly changing. Because there is no overall editorial oversight of the information available on the Internet, you must evaluate the accuracy and scope of that information yourself. For these and other reasons, it is a good idea to use the Internet as a supplement to traditional research methods.

Guidelines

Many of the larger foundations, as well as community foundations, issue guidelines, sometimes in pamphlet form but often as a section of their annual report. More than 1,650 foundations now have Web sites, where guidelines are often posted. Many more are likely to have Web sites in the near future. Foundation trustees and staff generally care deeply about the problems of society and struggle to determine the most effective strategies they can use to produce the greatest impact with their funding dollars. When they issue guidelines or announce areas of programmatic interests, these are the result of careful planning and strategy. You should thoroughly review any available guidelines as part of your investigation of a foundation or corporate donor. Some guidelines are very specific, stating goals or even projects to be funded within each area of interest. Others are more general and require further investigation.

If the foundation in question supports only medical research in Kenya, and your agency provides after-school reading programs for children in Columbus, Ohio, obviously, this is not a good prospect. However, if you are doing medical research at Stanford University that has implications for the population in Africa, there is a chance that the foundation might be interested in your work, if not now, then perhaps in the future.

Don't assume that a funder's guidelines from two years ago are still applicable today, particularly when a funder's assets are growing rapidly or it is experiencing a change in leadership. While the foundation probably will not shift its area of interest overnight from the arts to medicine, there may well be subtle changes in emphasis. You need to be aware of these before making your request.

For information on grants available, you should refer to requests for proposals (RFPs), an increasingly popular vehicle for foundations to publicize new program initiatives. Links to recently posted foundation RFPs are a feature of *Philanthropy News Digest* at the Center's Web site. The Center's RFP Bulletin is a weekly listing of current funding opportunities offered by foundations and grantmaking organizations and is delivered to your e-mail box at no charge.

Foundation Web Sites

Today more and more foundations and corporate giving programs have a presence on the Internet. The Foundation Center's Web site currently provides a comprehensive list of annotated links to the Web sites of foundations, corporate grantmakers, and grantmaking public charities. While the vast majority of foundations do not yet have Web sites, those that do maintain Web sites provide much of the information grantseekers have come to expect from print sources, such as annual reports, grants lists, application guidelines, and so forth. Some foundations post their annual reports *only* on the Web. Quite unlike the scenario when the previous edition of this *Guide* was published in 1997, all of the 39 grantmakers interviewed for this revision indicated either that they have a Web site or are in the process of creating one. Foundations are making enormous strides in the technological milieu, and grantseekers should be sure to explore existing and emerging Web resources.

The Foundation Center helps grantseekers identify which foundations and corporate giving programs have Web sites by two means. First, the Center's own Web site has links to the home pages of foundations or corporate giving programs that have Web sites. Second, *FC Search: The Foundation Center's Database on CD-ROM* allows you to link directly from a grantmaker record to its Web site.

The Annual Report

A foundation's annual report may prove to be a valuable tool in researching a funder. It is important not only for determining current giving patterns but also for projecting future trends. The annual report reflects the personality, style, and interests of the foundation.

In reading an annual report, you should look most closely at two sections. First, read the statement by the chairman, president, or chief executive. Look for clues that reveal the foundation's underlying philosophy. What are the problems in society that the foundation wants to address? What kind of impact does its leadership hope to make with the foundation's funds? This section will also reveal if the foundation is in the process of changing direction. Such a shift presents you with a significant window of opportunity, if your project happens to fit within new areas the foundation wants to explore.

The other section to examine is the list of grantees for the past year or years. Check the grants list against what the foundation *says* it wants to fund. You are looking for clues that will illustrate specific areas of interest. You also want to look for any discrepancies. Do they say, for instance, that they don't fund capital campaigns, yet right there listed in the grants list is a donation of $75,000 to the St. Clairesville Community Center to build a new gymnasium? This doesn't necessarily mean that you should keep them on your prospect list for your own gymnasium. It does mean that you should research the foundation further. Many foundations fund projects or agencies with special connections to the foundation or in which their trustees have a particular interest even though they fall outside their stated guidelines.

The 990-PF will not give you as much information about a foundation as guidelines or an annual report will, but if those are lacking, it is the place you can turn to find a foundation's grants list. For small, locally oriented foundations, the 990-PF may be the *only* source of details on grants awarded, because only about 1,400 foundations issue separate annual reports.

Refine

With information in hand about each foundation or corporation on your original list, you should refine your prospect list. Take care at this stage to focus only on those sources that are *most likely* to help your nonprofit now or in the future. Then ask yourself:

- Have I developed a thorough, well-rounded prospect list?
- Is it manageable? Given the need and the time I have to devote to fundraising, is the list too long or too short?

As you winnow your list, one question will arise: Does my project need to fit precisely within a funder's stated guidelines? Guidelines often indicate a particular area of interest, but they should not be viewed as definitive restrictions. A funder may be looking into changing its areas of support precisely at the time your proposal arrives; or someone at the foundation might evince some special interest in your project. Each foundation or corporate funder is unique and responds accordingly. Andrew Lark of the Frances L. and Edwin L. Cummings Memorial Fund notes, "Every foundation has its own personality. Research is critical." Use your common sense when determining whether it is too much of a stretch to go to the next step in exploring a particular funder.

11

Contacting and Cultivating Potential Funders

Making the Initial Contact

Once you have determined that a foundation is a likely funder, then you must initiate contact. Some foundations prefer that you call first to see if your project fits their specific guidelines. Be aware, however, that this is not a popular step with all funders.

If you decide to call first, be sure you don't appear to be going on a fishing expedition. Funders find this particularly annoying. Your conversation needs to make it clear that you have read the guidelines and want further clarification on whether your particular project would fit. You are *not* making a solicitation by telephone.

Funders caution that, if you do call, listen carefully to what is being said. Ilene Mack of the William Randolph Hearst Foundation commented, "I am happy to have a conversation with a grantseeker.

This way I can understand what kind of organization they are and if we are an appropriate fit."

On the other hand, Ms. Mack also cautions the grantseeker to be careful to "listen for the 'no.' "

There are three objectives to the initial call:

- It promotes name recognition of your group.
- It tests the possible compatibility between the potential funder and your agency.
- It permits you to gather additional information about the funder and about possible reaction to your project *before* you actually submit your proposal.

How should you proceed? First, rehearse what you will say about your organization. You may be given just a few minutes by the foundation or corporate representative. Also, have on hand the background information you have compiled about the potential funder and how much and what you would like them to fund. If there is a prior relationship with your nonprofit group, be fully aware of the details.

Second, make the call. It would be great if you could speak directly with the president of the foundation or senior vice president in charge of corporate contributions. But this will not often happen. Be satisfied with anyone who can respond to your questions. In the process, don't underestimate the importance of support staff. They can be very helpful. They can provide you with key information and ensure that your proposal is processed promptly. Be sure to obtain the name of the person you do speak with so that reference to this conversation can be made when you submit your formal request. This may be your contact person for future calls and letters.

What should you say? Be prepared to:

- Introduce your agency: give the name, location, purpose, and goals.
- State up front why you are calling: you want to learn more about this funder with the ultimate purpose of obtaining financial support.
- Inquire if you can submit a proposal: be specific about which one and the hoped-for level of support.

- Request an appointment: few funders are willing to grant the request for a meeting without at least an initial proposal on the table, but it's always worth inquiring about this. As a matter of fact, each time you speak with a funder, you should ask if a face-to-face conversation would be appropriate.

Variations will emerge in each call, so you must be sharp, alert, and ready to respond. At the same time, try to seem relaxed and confident as the discussion proceeds. Remember that you are a potential partner for the prospective funder.

Many foundations have no staff or limited office support. Some corporations assign their philanthropic activities to executives with very heavy workloads. The point is, repeated calls may go unanswered. Above all, be persistent. Persistence will set your agency apart from many nonprofits whose leaders initiate fundraising with determination but quickly lose heart. If you cannot get through to a potential funder on the telephone, send a letter of inquiry designed to gain the same information as the call. If your letter goes unanswered, then be prepared to submit a request anyway.

While some program officers will not meet with applicants until a proposal has been submitted, others say that they would prefer the proposal to be submitted only after a meeting. John Marshall of the Kresge Foundation points out, "We will help determine eligibility via the telephone. More importantly, we are willing to meet before a proposal is submitted to us and do so with upwards of 500 scheduled appointments per year."

The message here is that, like people, every foundation is different. Foundations, in fact, are made up of people. It is important to listen to and to respect what the funding representative is telling you about preferred styles of approach.

The Letter of Intent

Many grantmakers today are requesting that applicants provide a brief letter of inquiry or intent about their project *before* submitting a complete proposal. Just like the introductory phone call, this letter is used by funders as a simple screening device, enabling the grantmaker to preclude submission of an inappropriate application and to encourage the submission of proposals with funding potential. It also enables those grants decision makers who prefer to be involved in the shaping of a proposal at the very earliest stages to do so. The letter of intent can be useful to the grantseeker, since it saves time compiling lengthy documents and attachments for proposals that are unlikely to be favorably received.

The increasingly common requirement to submit a preliminary letter of intent is not always viewed favorably by the grantseeker. In the first place, it is an extra step, requiring that additional time be factored into the application cycle. Second, some view this procedure as a way for the funder to cut off an application before the grantseeker has had the opportunity to fully portray the benefits of the project. And finally, you need to have the full proposal, at least in draft form, before you can submit a letter of intent, which in a sense is a highly compacted proposal with most of the components covered, albeit briefly.

A talent for précis writing is definitely required to get the letter of intent just right. It should not be longer than two to three pages.

What follows is a letter of intent from the DC Heritage Tourism Coalition to the Eugene and Agnes E. Meyer Foundation:

Ms. Kathy Freshley
Eugene and Agnes E. Meyer Foundation
1400 16th Street NW, Suite 360
Washington, DC 20036

Dear Kathy:
I am writing on behalf of the DC Heritage Tourism Coalition to ask if we might submit a $75,000 operating support proposal to the Foundation for your March deadline.

The Eugene and Agnes E. Meyer Foundation has backed the Coalition since its inception. During the past year, its contributions have extended far beyond its $70,000 financial investment. Its confidence in our potential importance for the city is the bedrock on which we have been able to build support from other local foundations. Along with the Fannie Mae Foundation and other local philanthropies, the Eugene and Agnes E. Meyer Foundation last year enabled us to hire veteran Washington historian and community activist Kathryn Schneider Smith as Executive Director and Barbara Wolfson, the Coalition's administrator prior to incorporation, as Deputy Director. With its help we have recently completed a

---

strategic three-year plan against which to measure our progress, and at this point, we are meeting our goals and objectives. It is our hope that the Foundation will wish to continue its leadership role in building the core operating resources of the Coalition for the duration of this three-year start-up period, in particular the development of staffing levels capable of achieving our long-range objectives.

The Heritage Tourism Coalition is a grassroots coalition of Washington's neighborhood, economic development, and cultural organizations. Its mission is to strengthen the image and economy of the District of Columbia by engaging visitors in the diverse heritage of the city beyond the federal monuments.

More than 21 million people visit the Mall every year with money in their pockets. Research tells us that 61% of these tourists are here in search of history and culture—part of the international phenomenon known as "heritage tourism." Yet most return home without discovering the cultural treasures in our urban neighborhoods. Our local museums and other heritage sites do not benefit from their visits, our neighborhood restaurants and shops do not see their dollars, and our city is deprived of valuable tax revenues. We are also missing the opportunity to show our guests that this is a beautiful, vibrant, and fascinating city with a rich history all its own—a good place to live and do business, and a nation's capital of which they can be proud. The Heritage Tourism Coalition is seizing this opportunity on behalf of its city.

Founded in 1996 as a joint program of the Humanities Council of DC and the Washington Historical Society, the Coalition became an independent corporation in March 1999. It now has 81 members including neighborhood associations, community development organizations, museums, libraries, neighborhood historical societies, religious institutions, arts organizations, parks and gardens, preservation groups, tourism industry representatives, and the city's tourism entities, Metro, the National Park Service, and the Smithsonian Institution. It is one of the most diverse and active coalitions in the city.

Since its inception, the Coalition has succeeded in making heritage tourism an integral component of the city's economic development plans and is recognized by the city and its tourism entities as the principal coordinator and catalyst for these initiatives. It has mobilized not only its grassroots membership but the public agencies and private interests involved in marketing the city and revitalizing its neighborhoods, building for the first time the kind of partnerships necessary for progress toward these goals. It has initiated a host of projects ranging from neighborhood tours to the publication *Capital Assets,* the city's first inventory of cultural attractions by neighborhood. This workbook has already become a valued resource for the government and tourism industry and is in its second printing.

Our most important goals for the next three years are to 1) create a marked heritage trails system for neighborhoods throughout the city, 2) develop new guided walking tours, 3) improve and enrich the training of tour guides, 4) implement plans for a heritage tourism/community development model in Shaw and commence its replication in other targeted neighborhoods, and 5) build an organization with the staffing level and resources needed to implement these plans.

In the year ahead, we will also conduct baseline market research on the nature, behavior, and preferences of potential audiences for heritage tourism in the District; the status and needs of member organizations; and current levels of tourism and economic activity in the targeted neighborhoods. Findings will guide our future projects and those of our members, as well as provide the mechanisms for measuring the outcome of heritage tourism initiatives on cultural sites, economic development, and job creation. In addition, we will develop a heritage tourism website with virtual neighborhood tours and links to related sites across the region.

Our development strategy is to obtain city funding to match contributions of local philanthropies and national foundation support to match the total level of local support. Groundwork for the first two components of this public-private partnership has been laid, and we are presently initiating our approach to national philanthropic partners interested in the start-up of a model program in the nation's capital.

The Fannie Mae, Public Welfare, Marpat, and Philip L. Graham foundations have made financial commitments totaling $125,000 for the current year. If encouraged to apply, we would ask the Meyer Foundation to renew its support with a grant of $75,000, again assuming its role as our leading "private" partner in the development of this model heritage tourism program for the city of Washington—the only grassroots heritage tourism program in the nation, and the first to combine heritage tourism with economic development and neighborhood revitalization.

Thank you for your consideration.

Sincerely,
Lynne Fitzhugh
Board of Directors

Some grantmakers will even accept the letter of intent via e-mail. What follows is the format used by the W. K. Kellogg Foundation:

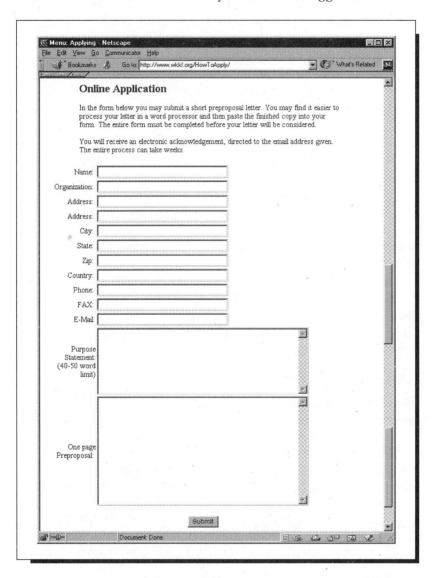

While the letter of intent has its pros and cons from the grantseeker's perspective, this is an increasingly popular vehicle among proposal reviewers. And writing such a letter is a skill that proposal writers need to develop.

Submitting the Proposal

Actually submitting the proposal may seem anticlimactic considering the amount of preparation that has gone into identifying and researching the prospective funders and putting together the various components. But once you have determined that a meeting prior to submission is not possible or is unnecessary, or once you've had the desired meeting, eventually there comes the time to submit the full proposal to the funders on your list.

Checklists may prove useful at this point. You may wish to check and double-check one last time to ensure that all requirements of the funder have been met and that all of the pieces of the proposal package are there in the proper sequence. Above all, you will want to be sure that you submit the proposal in accordance with the funder's deadline. If possible, whether you use regular mail, e-mail, or are applying online, send in your proposal at least two weeks in advance of the deadline. This enables the funder to request additional information, if needed.

Grantseekers often wonder whether they should mail in their proposals, send by overnight mail or messenger, or hand-deliver them. By far the best choice is the least expensive one. Use regular mail unless there is a very good reason to do otherwise.

Cultivating the Potential Funder

Don't forget to continue to communicate once you have submitted your proposal. Cultivation of the funding prospect can make the critical difference between getting a grant and getting lost in the shuffle.

Knowledge of the funder's situation, and of that particular grantmaker's procedures for processing proposals, can be extremely helpful in developing your cultivation strategy.

Funders are flooded with proposals. Even if they turn down all that are clearly outside their guidelines, they still get many more than their budgets will allow them to fund. Ruth Shack of Dade Community Foundation notes, "We get three times as many requests as we have resources." And Roxanne Ford of W.M. Keck Foundation points out, "In our prior year, we had 2,700 contacts. We met with 213 nonprofits, did 56 grant visits, and made 53 grants."

How can you assure that your proposal will be one of those to get into the grant pipeline? The ways in which foundations operate differ widely. At some small family foundations, the donor himself or herself will review all requests. At the larger foundations, a first cut is usually made to eliminate those that are out of program, then program officers review proposals in specific areas and must take each proposal through a staff review process before a recommendation goes to their board of trustees. Andrew Lark describes the Frances L. & Edwin L. Cummings Memorial Fund's process as follows: "There is an immediate rejection if a request is out of our funding guidelines. We generally ask those being considered to fill out a Cummings Fund questionnaire form. Then we do site visits. We look for efficiency in the way they run the program, realism in the application, and strong board/management involvement."

Foundations frequently work closely with the grantseeker in developing the request. As Eugene Wilson of the Ewing Marion Kauffman Foundation points out, "If the proposal is considered for an award, there will be a lot of interaction. Our staff is very involved with our applicants and grantees - people working together to solve problems." And Susan Lajoie Eagan of the Cleveland Foundation notes: "A program officer will follow up, offering guidance regarding the proposal submission."

Peter Bird of the Frist Foundation gives this overview: "The proposal is not the first step, but the last. We get to know the community's needs: read, talk, be well informed, be receptive. It is a grantseeker's job to assess the community's needs and find out what the grantmaker wants. A funder should be open and flexible, not tightly drawn."

John Marshall of the Kresge Foundation summarizes the challenge facing nonprofit grantseekers: "Agencies have to make informed choices about the sources to which they will apply. Then they need to follow that up with good communication and a carefully constructed application. Speed doesn't take the place of judgment."

Several forms of cultivation may be particularly valuable after the proposal is submitted:

- Communication by phone or e-mail;
- Face-to-face meetings;
- Using board contacts; and
- Written updates and progress reports.

Communication by Phone or E-mail

Normally you should plan to call or send an e-mail about two weeks after the proposal package is mailed. The primary purpose of this communication is to make sure that the proposal has been received. You have requested a meeting in the cover letter and offered to supply any additional information required to help the funder consider your request. You should therefore ask if it is appropriate to schedule a meeting at the foundation or corporate office or a site visit at your agency. Be sure to ask about the process and timing for the review of your proposal. This will guide you as to when you might call back or send updated information.

Call periodically thereafter to check on the status of your proposal. If you have had no response in the expected time frame, call to find out if there has been a change in the schedule. Ask the same types of questions as you did previously: Is additional information required? When will the proposal be reviewed? Would the foundation or corporate representative like to meet? Be brief. There is a fine line between being helpful and being too pushy.

Each time you call, be prepared to answer the program officer's detailed questions about any aspect of the proposal or of your agency's work. You should also expect to receive calls or e-mails from your program officer during the course of the proposal review.

Hunter Corbin of the Hyde and Watson Foundation warns the grantseeker that it frustrates the funder "when you call the nonprofit, and no one knows what the application is all about. Worse, you call the organization and request information, and no one calls you back."

It helps to stay in touch by phone or e-mail. This gives you a chance to find out what is happening with your proposal and to share information with the foundation or corporate funder.

When appropriate, follow up the phone conversation with a note or e-mail message about the next step you plan to take or confirming any new information you provided over the phone. While phone communication is often the most convenient way to keep in touch, you need to be sure that any agreement or information that is critical to a successful outcome of the review process is put in writing.

Face-to-Face Meetings

Appointments can be very hard to obtain. Many funders will not agree to a meeting until the proposal is under active consideration.

This might entail assigning it to a program officer, who would then be the person to meet with you. Even when the foundation or corporate representative respects your group or is intensely interested in your project, he or she may believe that a meeting would not be helpful in arriving at a recommendation on your request. However, some foundations insist on a site visit for most or all of the groups to which they make grants.

When you are offered an appointment, you should view this as a very special opportunity. It is one that you must prepare for carefully.

First, be sure that the right team is selected to attend the meeting. If your nonprofit agency has staff, the chief executive officer or executive director should go. The CEO should be able to answer specific questions relating to the project. The other member of the team should be a volunteer, preferably from the board. The presence of the volunteer underscores the fact that the board is aware of and supports the work of the organization. Under the right circumstances, a member of the program staff can be a helpful adjunct, or you must bring along someone who benefits from the good work of your organization. But don't overwhelm the funder by bringing too many additional people to the meeting. John Murphy of the Flinn Foundation has this to say, "Send me the people who are doing the work, not the fundraiser." Clear with the funding representative precisely how many people are welcome. If time permits, call a day in advance to confirm the date and remind the funder who is coming. Invite the prospective funder to visit your organization. A site visit obviously allows you to introduce the funding representative to a wider range of people involved in your agency or project.

Next, prepare for the meeting. Compile background information about the foundation or corporation. You should be careful to note any prior interaction with the funder, especially if it was less than positive. Develop a profile of the person(s) with whom you are meeting, if this information is available in standard biographical sources, on the Web, or via the grapevine. Your peers in the nonprofit world who are grant recipients might shed some light on the personality and idiosyncrasies of the funder.

Create a role for each of the participants. It is critical that no one sits idle. There should be a dialogue and rapport among the meeting participants.

Last, know precisely what you want to accomplish in the meeting. You won't leave with a check in hand, but you do need to decide in advance what information you want to share and to obtain.

You should expect to accomplish a great deal through the simple process of meeting face-to-face with the funder. The meeting will establish a personal relationship between the representatives of your organization and of the funding agency. Despite our high-tech world, giving is still a highly personal activity. Hence, the better your rapport with the donor, the more likely it is that financial support will be forthcoming.

Along with getting to know the people at your agency, this will be an opportunity for the funding representative to gain a much better understanding of your group's work. Hearing from knowledgeable people about your mission, programs, and dreams will allow the funder to ask questions, to refine information, and to correct misperceptions.

Equally important, the funder will gain a much better sense of the project for which you are seeking support. Critical information about the proposal, such as the need, methods for addressing it, and the capability of your group to run the program, might be covered during discussion. For this reason, be sure to review the proposal carefully before the meeting.

You must assume responsibility for the agenda of the meeting. Be prepared to:

- Use an icebreaker. The first few times you attend a meeting with a funder, it can be nerve-racking. Break the tension by telling an amusing anecdote, by relaying a true incident of interest to the group, or by commenting about the view or an object in the room where the meeting takes place.

- Introduce all of the meeting participants by name, title, and/or role. This way the funder will know the players and be clear to whom specific questions should be addressed.

- Get down to business. Once introduced, the participants should promptly move on to the real purpose of the meeting: your group hopes the funder will become a partner with you in getting your project off the ground.

- Remind the funder about the mission and history of your agency. Be thorough but brief in this review.

- Describe the programs you offer. Again, be succinct, but be certain that the funder has a good overview of your services. This is important in case the project submitted for funding proves not to be of interest. The funder may request a proposal relating to a different aspect of your agency's work, having achieved a good grasp of the whole program.

- Describe the project for which you are seeking support. It is critical that you demonstrate the conviction that success is likely. Provide the necessary detail for the funder to understand the problem being addressed and your agency's proposed response to it.

- Keep a dialogue going. It is easy to speak at length about your organization. But it is also easy to bore the funders and, even worse, for you to come away from the meeting not having gained any relevant new information about this grantmaker. Whenever possible, try to elicit the funder's reactions. Inquire about current programs they have funded that address similar problems. Treat the grantmaker as a potential partner. Remember, their dollars have significance only when combined with programs. Listen carefully to their responses, comments, and questions. This dialogue will clue you into the *real* interests and concerns of this potential funder. Don't assume anything.

- Obtain a clear understanding of the next steps. You should determine the following: if anything more is needed for review of the request; when the proposal will come up for review; and how the agency will be notified about the outcome. If, as a result of this conversation, it is clear that the proposal is unlikely to be funded, you should ask what you might do to resubmit this or another proposal.

A great deal can be accomplished in a well-crafted meeting, whether at their place or yours. You don't want this process spoiled by extending it for too long. Once it is clear that the objectives have been achieved, you need to summarize the next steps to be taken by both sides and move on to a cordial goodbye. End the meeting while the "good vibes" are still being felt by both sides.

Using Board Contacts

A contact from one of your board members with a peer affiliated with the foundation or corporate funder you are approaching will usually reinforce the relationship you are building.

How do you discover if your board members have contacts that can help with raising funds? First, circulate to all of the members of your board the names of the officers and directors of the foundations and corporations you plan to approach. Ask your board members to respond to you by a certain date about those whom they know. Then work one-on-one with individual board members, building a strategy for them to utilize their contacts. Another approach is to meet with the board members to talk about individuals with whom they can be helpful. You may find contacts with funders that you had not intended to approach, where having an entree will make a difference.

Knowing that you have board-to-board contact is not enough. You must assist your board member in capitalizing on this relationship on behalf of your nonprofit group. First, develop a scenario with the board member focusing on how to approach the contact. The more personal the approach, the better it is. Second, assist your board member with understanding why this funder would want to help your organization, finding the right language to discuss your agency and your funding needs, and drafting correspondence as needed. Then make sure that the board member makes the promised contact. Periodically remind this individual of the next step to be taken. The groundwork you have done is wasted if the board member never follows through.

Be forewarned that staff of foundations and corporate grant-makers may be concerned about your board members contacting their board members. This is particularly true of professionally staffed foundations where program officers may consider it inappropriate or may view it as interference. Some funders feel strongly that an agency should not use a board contact, even if they have one.

Still others report that their trustees are encouraged to indicate their interest in a project. At a minimum, staff want to know in advance that a board contact will be used. Julie Rogers of the Eugene and Agnes E. Meyer Foundation advises, "Let the staff know that this is happening—give them a 'heads up.' This is smart human relations."

Where you already are in contact with the foundation staff, it is critical to discuss a board contact with them before it is set in motion. Finally, keep in mind that relying on board contacts can backfire. At some foundations, if a board member has had contact with an agency, he or she is expected to disqualify himself from discussion about the specific proposal.

Written Updates and Progress Reports

Written communication helps a foundation or corporate donor learn more about your group and reminds them that you need their support. You should plan to send materials selectively while your proposal is under review. Here are some ideas for what you might send:

- summary reports on what is going on in your organization;
- financial information, such as a new audit;
- newsletters, bulletins, brochures, or other frequently issued information;
- updates/reports on specific projects; and
- newspaper or magazine articles on the project for which you have requested support, the work of your nonprofit, or closely related issues.

It is usually not necessary to customize the materials, but a brief accompanying note always helps to reinforce your relationship with the funder.

Here are three examples of update letters:

Mr. Alfredo A. Cruz
John S. and James L. Knight Foundation
One Biscayne Tower, Suite 3800
2 South Biscayne Blvd.
Miami, FL 33131-1803

Dear Mr. Cruz:

Following is an updated report on pledges and gifts to the Detroit Zoological Society's capital campaign. Commitments from private sources now total $12,709,257. This figure includes five new gifts from Board members totaling more than $82,000, which were secured after we submitted our proposal to the Knight Foundation.

During September, we were active in our cultivation and solicitation of all remaining members of our Board, and we submitted a $2-million capital request to The Skillman Foundation. We expect this proposal to be reviewed in December. A matured bequest of more than $100,000 is anticipated in early 2000 and will be credited to the campaign.

Grants from our State and City governments remain at $3.9 million. We are confident that we will receive additional support from the City of Detroit in the next fiscal year. It also appears likely that the State of Michigan will consider an additional grant before year-end.

Public and private support for the Detroit Zoological Society's capital campaign totals $16,609,257 to date. If you have any further questions about campaign progress or our proposal to the Knight Foundation, please do not hesitate to contact me again. Thank you for your attention to our request and for your thoughtful consideration.

Sincerely,

Jane Alessandrini
Director of Development

Cynthia D. Robbins
Senior Program Officer
Eugene and Agnes E. Meyer Foundation
1400 16th Street, NW, Suite 360
Washington, DC 20036

Dear Cynthia:

We want to thank you for taking the time out of your busy
schedule to join us for the Community IMPACT! Donor Forum.
It is our hope that you walked away with a better understanding of our model and a clear picture of our effort to deepen our
work around youth/adult partnerships for social change in DC.

We certainly value the group's comments, insights, and suggestions. We rely on the DC funding community not only for its
financial resources but also for its feedback that helps make our
programs more effective.

This Forum will be an ongoing event, and we plan to host
the next one in the fall. At that time, we will update you on the
progress of this initiative and its desired outcomes.

Thank you again for attending. Your support is critical to
helping change the nation's capital, one neighborhood at a time.

Sincerely,

Greg Taylor
Executive Director

Tom Waters
Development Director

Mr. David Nasby
General Mills Foundation
PO Box 1113
Minneapolis, MN 55440

Dear Dave:

We write to you today as excited board members for the Ballet of the Dolls. We thought this would be a great time to update you on what is happening with the Dolls. Some of it is challenging, yet for the most part it is exhilarating.

Our FY 2000 recently ended, and unfortunately we ended it with roughly a $53,000 deficit. Though a deficit of this size concerns us, it does not hamper our spirits. Quite the opposite. The board has recently approved a well-crafted budget for FY 2001. The earned income is conservative; the contributed income is aggressive without being unrealistic; and the expenses are tight but still allow us to produce quality dance as we have for the past ten years. Myron Johnson, Craig Harris, and our executive committee worked hard on the number crunching. The result is a budget that will benefit the Dolls greatly during this period of change.

We anticipate at least a $22,000 surplus for FY 2001, which will be used to diminish our liabilities. The board is committed to working diligently at fundraising this year. We are creating a strong development committee headed by the two of us and involving four or five other board members and a few community members. Our goal is to surplus all of the budgeted contributed income figures.

The board is also looking to double its size over the next year. The initial response from prospective board members is thrilling. Even when they hear we have a deficit to overcome, people are still excited to join us in our work. Though board building takes time, we feel that in a year we will have one of the strongest arts boards in town.

We look forward to telling you more about this incredible community asset, the Ballet of the Dolls, as the year progresses. If in the meantime you have any questions or comments, please feel free to call either of us.

Sincerely,

Theresa Parker   Bill Venne
Development Chair   Development Vice-Chair

E-mail Communication

Don't overlook the possibility of selective e-mail communiqués with prospective funders, if they have communicated with you that way in the past or have indicated a preference for this vehicle for providing updates. A concise e-mail message with, perhaps, a link to an appropriate area of your Web site or other Internet coverage of your activities, can have a significant impact. Repeated or unnecessary e-mail messages directed at funding program officers can prove annoying, however.

Some agencies have developed listservs or broadcast e-mail services to keep various constituents apprised of recent developments. It would be wise *not* to add a funder's e-mail address to your listserv without prior permission to do so. On the other hand, this is a very convenient way to keep donors and prospective funders aware of your agency's accomplishments.

Even after your project has concluded, don't forget to continue to cultivate your donors. Fundraising is all about relationship building. In the words of Joel Orosz of the W. K. Kellogg Foundation, "We expect to stay in touch with former grantees. Sometimes as a result of communication with them, an idea surfaces in which we have an interest. If this happens, we will encourage the submission of a proposal."

12

Life after the Grant — or Rejection

The Initial Follow-up to a Grant

You've just received a grant from a foundation or corporation. Congratulations! What should you do? First of all, you should celebrate. Include everyone in your agency who contributed to this wonderful outcome. Thank them for their help and remind them about what this means for your organization.

Next, send a thank-you letter to your funder. This seems so obvious that one would think it hardly worth stating. Yet a number of the grantmakers interviewed for this book responded to the question, "What is the best thing an organization can do after receiving a grant?" with the simple response: send a thank-you letter. Here are two samples.

Ms. Julie Rogers
President
Eugene and Agnes E. Meyer Foundation
1400 16th Street, NW, Suite 360
Washington, DC 20036

Dear Ms. Rogers:

On behalf of the Board of Directors, the staff, and membership of the District of Columbia Arts Center, I want to thank you for awarding us a $20,000 challenge grant. Our board is enthused at the prospect of meeting another challenge and looks forward to working with the Meyer Foundation yet again this year. Last year's challenge was a terrific shot in the arm for our organization, and we are committed to demonstrating our capacity to meet the challenge again this year.

I would particularly like to thank Kathy Freshley for her cooperation with us in preparing this proposal and her continuing support of the District of Columbia Arts Center. She has proven to be a good friend to our organization, and she is a wonderful representative for the Meyer Foundation.

Sincerely,
B. Stanley
Executive Director

Mr. John H. Clymer, Chair
Hyams Foundation
175 Federal Street
Boston, MA 02110

Dear Mr. Clymer:

On behalf of the MYTOWN staff and Board of Directors, thank you for the Hyams Foundation grant of $40,000 to support operating expenses for FY 1999 and 2000. This investment will allow MYTOWN to continue its two-prong civic effort to educate Boston residents about the city's rich multi-ethnic heritage and to develop young citizens committed to local history and community activism.

Hyams distinguishes itself as a founding member of MYTOWN's family of supporters: civic-minded corporations, foundations, and residents collectively working to keep high-content, high-quality cultural learning opportunities affordable and accessible for all of Boston. Thank you for believing in us and the work that we are committed to doing for this city. Together we are making a difference.

Again, thank you for your continued support. We look forward to another exciting season together.

Sincerely yours,

Karilyn Crockett
Co-Director & Co-Founder

P.S. We extend a warm invitation for all Hyams staff and families to join us this spring for a 2000 Season MYTOWN walking tour.

The foundation representatives we interviewed expressed a concern that needs to be taken to heart. Appreciate the investment that has just been made in your agency. Recognize that it is not just an institution that is supporting you but the actual people within that institution. Remember that the grants decision makers feel good about the decision to invest in your organization. They may even have had to fight for you in the face of opposition by other staff and board members. Show your thanks and appreciation for this vote of confidence.

Grantmakers want to ensure effective communication after a grant is awarded. They remind us that a grant is a contract to undertake a specific set of activities, and they want and need to know what has transpired.

Remember the watchword of all fundraising: communication. A telephone call to say "Thank you," an update on recent activities, or an announcement of additional funding committed or received are all ways to keep in touch after the grant is made.

Grant Reporting

If a foundation has specific reporting requirements, you will be told what they are. Usually reporting requirements are included in the grant letter; sometimes you are asked to sign and return a copy of the grant letter or of a separate grant contract. These "conditions," which a representative of the nonprofit signs, sometimes require timely reports that are tied to payments.

Here is the Conditions of Grant and Request for Payment form which describes the Flinn Foundation's legal and reporting conditions:

Flinn Foundation
Conditions of Grant and Request for Payment Form

For the Foundation to proceed with payment of the grant funds authorized, the Conditions of Grant statement must be reviewed and the Request for Payment Form signed by the recipient organization's chief officer, and returned to the Foundation. Signature of this form by the chief officer of a grantee organization (CEO, dean of school or head of an academic unit) constitutes review and acceptance of the conditions specified.

Initial payment of grant funds (generally, two payments on grants of up to $25,000 or less; no more than the first three months of project activity costs of multi-year grants) will be made upon presentation of this signed and completed form to the Foundation, plus submission by the project director (the individual directly responsible for developing and guiding the funded activity) of a project implementation schedule and budget detailing how these initial grant funds will be spent.

Evidence of readiness to initiate project activity in keeping with the intent of the grant award must be submitted for the Foundation to release grant funds. If a significant portion of grant funds are to be used to pay the salary of professional staff not yet hired or to pay the contract of a consultant or vendor, the project director must submit documentation of the employee hire (CV and start date) and/or copies of the signed and dated contracts with consultants or vendors before initial payment will be made.

These documents will be reviewed by Foundation staff and, if found to be consistent with the intent of the grant, payment will be made within thirty (30) days of receipt. All grant payment checks will be mailed by the Foundation to the address shown on this form. No grant checks will be delivered personally nor, for security purposes, will a grant payment check be released to any representative of the grantee organization.

Subsequent payments on multi-year grants and those in excess of $25,000 will be made upon submission by the project director of a line-item expenditure report detailing how initial grant funds were spent. This report should also specify the amount of grant funds needed to support project activity for the subsequent time period. A brief narrative report prepared by the project director, which describes project activity for that time period, must also be submitted with this expenditure report.

Foundation Grant ID number_____

Institutional Grant ID number _____

Duration of Grant Period (total project length):

From _____through _____
       (month, day, year)   (month, day, year)

Total Amount of Approved Grant: $_____

Amount of first payment: $_____ Date Requested:_____

Check to be made payable to: _____

Check to be mailed to (name, title, address): _____

Project Director (name, title, address, telephone, e-mail address): _____

Institutional Project Fiscal Officer (name, title, address, telephone, e-mail address): _____

The conditions of the grant are hereby accepted and agreed to as of the date specified.

By: _____
       (organization's principal officer)

Title: _____

Date: _____

Here is an example of how the Hyde and Watson Foundation communicates with grantees.

Ladies and Gentlemen:

It is a pleasure to inform you that in response to an appeal dated September 6, 2000, a grant was authorized on October 18, 2000, as specified below:

Grantee: _____
Grant Purpose: Purchase of books and instructional tools
Grant Amount: $10,000.00

This grant was voted payable in the year ending 2000. Enclosed is a check for $10,000.00 which represents payment in full. **By the act of accepting, endorsing, and depositing the check, you confirm the following four statements:**

1. That this Foundation does not control the above-mentioned grantee organization, its projects, or programs;

2. That the grantee organization listed above continues to be tax exempt under Section 501(c)(3) and is "not a private foundation" under Section 509(a) of the Internal Revenue Code (or other appropriate ruling);

3. That the grant funds will not be used in any way which would subject this grantor Foundation to penalty taxes;

4. That a grant/progress report will be forwarded to us as soon as the funds are expended or no later than one year from the date of the enclosed check.

Please note that the grant report (Item 4) is very important. In accordance with our current guidelines, future proposals will be considered at the Grants Committee/Board level only after the required report including confirmation of expenditures of the funds has been received. The report should include the following information:

- A statement confirming that the grant funds have been expended in accordance with the terms of the grant;

- A brief to moderate narrative on the grant project including a statement as to what impact the grant had on the organization and the project itself, along with a financial breakdown of how the grant funds were spent.

On behalf of the Board of Directors of this Foundation, I wish you much success with your endeavors.

Sincerely yours,

Hunter W. Corbin
President

When a foundation provides formal reporting guidelines, in most cases there will be dates when the reports are due. If they have given you specific dates for reporting, develop a tickler system to keep track of them. If you can tell now that you'll have a problem meeting these deadlines (such as your auditors are scheduled for March, and the audited financial report is due in February), discuss this with the funder immediately. If the foundation staff has not heard from the grantee within a reasonable time period after the reports are due, they will call or send the grant recipient a note to follow up.

Some funders want reports at quarterly or six-month intervals, but most request an annual report and/or a final report, two to three months after the conclusion of the project. Even for grants of fairly short duration, foundations often express the desire to receive an interim report. Unless otherwise stated, an interim report can be informal.

The Cleveland Foundation issues very specific reporting instructions. Their *Grant Report Preparation Guidelines* provide a useful framework to guide agency staff in drafting a report to *any* funder. While these guidelines are designed for the Cleveland Foundation's grantees, they provide a reliable model for reports to other foundations that may not be as specific in their requirements.

The following guidelines are reprinted in their totality with permission from the Cleveland Foundation:

THE CLEVELAND FOUNDATION
GRANT REPORT PREPARATION GUIDELINES

OVERVIEW

In accordance with its Grant Agreement, The Cleveland Foundation requires all grant recipients to prepare periodic narrative and financial reports on project activity and expenditures corresponding to the project's approved budget.

Periodic reports are not only necessary for proper oversight to ensure accountability, but also serve as a valuable learning tool for both Foundation staff and grantees. We greatly appreciate your candor and thoughtful review of your project experience. Be assured that we do not share these documents with any other organization or funder. Please follow the guidelines below carefully.

NARRATIVE AND FINANCIAL REPORTS

- Please refer to **Section 2** of your Grant Agreement for the scheduled due dates of your reports.

- Use the attached forms for both interim and final reports.

- Type your reports and answer all questions in the order listed. **Please complete and attach the information cover sheet to your report.** We suggest that your response not exceed five pages.

- The financial report should include expenditures incurred as well as the balance of Foundation funds unexpended through the reporting period. Use parentheses to indicate any budget deficits in the "Balance" column of the form. Each financial report should be signed by the grantee's chief financial officer or chief executive officer.

- Final reports should include a review of performance and activities covering the entire grant period.

- **Please return two copies of the signed and dated narrative and financial reports in the same envelope.**

RELEASE OF GRANT FUNDS
The Foundation may hold scheduled grant payments until it has received properly completed narrative and financial grant reports. Please refer to **Section 5** of the Grant Agreement for more information concerning the release of grant funds.

UNEXPENDED FUNDS
Funds that are not expended or encumbered during the grant period should be returned to The Cleveland Foundation unless the Foundation makes written authorization to extend the award beyond the original end date of the grant.

THE CLEVELAND FOUNDATION
GRANT REPORT INFORMATION COVER SHEET

(Please feel free to retype or make copies of this information page)

Please check one: ❑ Interim Report   ❑ Final Report

Dates Covered By This Report: From _____ To _____

Grant Number _____

Name of Organization _____

Address _____

Project Director _____

Phone Number _____

Start Date of Grant Period _____

End Date of Grant Period _____

Grant Amount _____

Purpose of Grant _____

Report Prepared by: _____
                    Date   Name (Type or Print)

Signature _____

Phone _____ FAX _____

THE CLEVELAND FOUNDATION
NARRATIVE REPORT

- **Please retype the headings and questions as provided.**

- Please answer all the questions in the order listed. Those questions not applicable to your project should be marked NA.

I. PROJECT INFORMATION
(If more appropriate, you may defer responding to questions five and six until the final report.)

1. Please summarize your original expected outcomes for this project and how you had planned to achieve them.

2. What have been the principal accomplishments of the project to date? How have they been achieved? How have the grant funds been used?

3. The Foundation recognizes that circumstances can change, possibly affecting project implementation. What, if any, difficulties have you encountered; why did they occur; and what refinements or plans have been made to overcome them? Please indicate activities that are behind schedule or not yet begun, and any changes in project plans or personnel.

4. What have been the most challenging or surprising aspects of this project? Have there been any unexpected outcomes?

5. Based on your experience to date, what advice would you give to other organizations planning a similar program? What have been the strengths and limitations of the project? What would you do differently if you had the chance?

6. Please describe your post-grant plans for this project. How will it be financed?

II. ORGANIZATIONAL INFORMATION

It is very helpful to understand the organizational context in which your project is proceeding. Please take this opportunity to update us on any significant organizational changes, developments or challenges. How have these developments contributed to or impeded the success of the project? Additionally, is there any problem or issue confronting your organization requiring technical assistance? If so, would a meeting with Foundation staff be helpful at this time?

III. ATTACHMENTS (optional)

Please attach copies of any public recognition, awards, press releases or news articles pertinent to this project.

THE CLEVELAND FOUNDATION
PROJECT FINANCIAL REPORT

(Please feel free to retype or make copies of this page)

Organization: _____

Project Title: _____

Grant Number: _____

❑ Interim Report   ❑ Final Report

Dates Covered By This Report: From _____ To _____

Line Item	Amount Approved	Amount Expended	Balance
Personnel Expenses	$ _____	$ _____	$ _____
Staff Costs	$ _____	$ _____	$ _____
Fringe Benefits	$ _____	$ _____	$ _____
Total Personnel Expenses	$ _____	$ _____	$ _____
Non-Personnel Expenses	$ _____	$ _____	$ _____
Contract Services	$ _____	$ _____	$ _____
Office Space	$ _____	$ _____	$ _____
Equipment/Supplies	$ _____	$ _____	$ _____
Travel/Related Expenses	$ _____	$ _____	$ _____
Other	$ _____	$ _____	$ _____
Total Non-Personnel Expenses	$ _____	$ _____	$ _____
Total Project Expenses	$ _____	$ _____	$ _____

Report Prepared By:
Name (Type or Print): _____

Date: _____   Signature: _____

Phone: _____   Fax: _____

The Cleveland Foundation guidelines are particularly applicable if you have received special project support. Don't be concerned if your project does not lend itself to many of these questions. For instance, if you have received $15,000 to hire a tutor for your after-school program, some of the sections are probably not applicable. Others, like post-grant plans, should be addressed in some fashion in almost any report.

Even if you have received unrestricted, general-purpose support, funders want to know what overall goals you set for your agency for the year. Did you achieve them? What were some specific triumphs? What were some particular problems you faced, and how did you overcome them? Or, are you still dealing with the challenges? (Remember, realism is what counts, along with a sense of confidence that you are appropriately managing the grant.) What follows is a report to the Hyde and Watson Foundation from the Long Island Fund for Women and Girls.

Hunter W. Corbin, President
The Hyde and Watson Foundation
437 Southern Boulevard
Chatham Township, NJ 07928

Dear Mr. Corbin:

This is the final report for the grant we received from your Foundation in 1998. The grant funded our organization with money to obtain two new computers, a laser printer, envelope feeder, and office furniture. To date we have accomplished the following:

- Purchased a Pentium II 350 MHZ computer with backup tape drive, zip drive and 17" monitor for $1,710

- Purchased a HP LaserJet printer 17ppm/1200dpi— network version for $1,420

- Obtained an executive work station for $550; 2 additional matching desks @$150 each, plus 3- year insurance coverage for damages—$60

- Purchased a Pentium III 500 MHZ computer with Microsoft Windows 98 Operating System, APC Back-UPS 500, Ethernet Hub (for the peer-to-peer network), 15" monitor, and 4 backup tapes for $1,733
- Purchased a HP 4000 Envelope Feeder for $294

We are located in donated office space from Briarcliffe College, a local business school. Staff at the college have donated their time to help set up our machines. With the money allocated for the services donated, we used the remainder of the grant to purchase a Pentium III and Envelope Feeder. The total cost of our equipment was $6,067. Your grant covered most of the total costs for our equipment, with the balance added by our organization.

With the purchase of this third computer, we were able to network the machines for greater efficiency. The college and a private consulting firm, Gateway Network Services (GNS), have continued to volunteer their time. Our mailing list is currently 4,500, and GNS is helping us to develop a comprehensive database so we can better organize our records. On March 1, 2000 we launched our website, thanks to the donated services of Long Island Web Developers Guild (a mentor/apprentice program) and WriteDesign, and we hope to soon develop an online clearinghouse/advocacy resource center as part of our Gender Equity in K–12 Education Project.

This grant has helped to strengthen our infrastructure, and we have been able to concentrate our efforts on outside needs. We appreciate the support.

Thank you again.

Sincerely,

Sherry Radowitz, Ph.D.
Executive Director

These are presented as general models only. If a foundation supplies its own guidelines for reporting, then adhere to those instructions.

Seeking a Renewal

In certain cases, you will want to request that the grant be renewed or that a follow-up project be supported. Some funders refuse to give renewed support because they do not want to encourage dependency or because they see their funding as providing "seed money."

Other funders require a certain period of time to elapse between the grant and the renewal request. For instance, the Hearst Foundations currently require three years between grants.

Even a grant that could be a candidate for renewal may be labeled a one-time gift. Ordinarily the phrase "one-time gift" means that the funder is making no commitment to future funding. It does not necessarily mean that no possibility for future support exists.

If you know that you will want to request renewed support, you should communicate this early on to the foundation in order to determine the best time to submit another request. Be careful not to wait too long before requesting a renewal. By the time the funder receives the request, all the foundation's funds may be committed for the following year.

You should also determine early on the format required by the funder for submitting a renewal request. Some foundations require a full proposal; others want just a letter. This is another illustration of the differences among funders. It reinforces the need to communicate with the grantmaker to determine its particular requirements.

A report on funds expended and results of the first grant is a particularly critical document if you are going to ask for renewed support. However, many funders want your request for renewal to be separate from the report on the grant. In larger foundations, the report and the request for renewal might be handled by different departments; therefore, if you submit your renewal request as part of the report on the first grant, it might not find its way into the proposal system.

Following Up on a Declination

The most important response to a rejection letter is not to take it personally. An old fundraising adage is that "Campaigns fail because people don't ask, not because they get rejected." If your proposal gets rejected, it means you are out there asking. You are doing what you should be doing. Hopefully, you have sent your proposal to a number of other appropriate funders and have not "put all your eggs in one basket." A rule of thumb is that you should approach three funders for every grant you need. Thus, even if one or two prospects turn your proposal down, you still have a shot at the third.

Some funders will talk with you about why the proposal was rejected, particularly if you had a meeting with the program staff at the granting institution prior to or at the time of submission. A phone call following a rejection letter can help you clarify the next step. Your request may have been of great interest to the foundation but was turned down in that funding cycle because the board had already committed all the funds set aside for projects in your subject or geographical area. For example, if your request was for an AIDS program in South Chicago, the foundation may have already committed its grants budget for that geographic area. A call to a foundation staff member might result in encouragement to reapply in a later funding cycle.

All funding representatives emphasize, however, the need to be courteous in the process of calling once you have received a rejection letter. It is never easy to say "no," and a program officer who fought hard for your proposal may feel almost as disappointed as you are that it was turned down. While foundation staff usually want to be helpful, it is important to recognize that it can often be difficult to tell someone why a proposal has been rejected.

Most of the grantmakers interviewed for this guide would agree with Hunter Corbin of the Hyde and Watson Foundation about turndowns. He said, "There may be a couple of factors, but the usual ones are:

- we run out of money;
- the timing of the application is off;
- the request is vague;
- we are not interested in the subject."

It is important to take your cue from the funder, either from the rejection letter or from the follow-up call to staff. If you are not encouraged to resubmit, then you probably shouldn't.

There are times when a funder will encourage you to resubmit the same request at a particular time in the future. If you have been given this advice, then follow it. In your cover letter, be sure to refer to your conversation with the funding representative, remembering to restate, but not overstate, the earlier conversation.

Even if a foundation is not interested in funding the particular project you submitted, by keeping the lines of communication open and remaining respectful you will be nurturing the opportunity for future funding. Hildy Simmons of J. P. Morgan Charitable Trust reminds us, "Remember, 'no' isn't forever. Be gracious about the turndown. It is okay to call or write for feedback."

What follows is a sample rejection letter/thank-you letter from Advocates for Children and Youth to the Eugene and Agnes E. Meyer Foundation.

Julie L. Rogers, President
The Eugene and Agnes E. Meyer Foundation
1400 Sixteenth Street, NW
Suite 360
Washington, DC 20036-2217

Dear Ms. Rogers:

I recently received notification that our proposal for a regional outreach coordinator for the Maryland Children's Action Network (MD CAN) was not selected for funding by the trustees of The Eugene and Agnes E. Meyer Foundation. We understand the limitations of funding and sincerely appreciate having had the opportunity to submit our request.

Since our concern and interests in improving the lives of families is mutual, we will continue to update you and the Foundation on ACY's and MD CAN's efforts and successes. Together, we will make a meaningful and measurable difference in the lives of Maryland's children.

Sincerely,

Jann Jackson
Executive Director

Summary Tips

What to do if you receive a grant:

- Send a personalized thank you.
- Keep the funder informed of your progress.
- Follow the funder's reporting requirements.

What to do if your request is turned down:

- Don't take it personally.
- Be sure you understand why.
- Find out if you can resubmit at a later date.

13

What the Funders Have to Say

Introduction

The number of interviewees for this edition increased dramatically from 21 in the prior edition of this book to 39 in the current edition. (For a complete list, see page vi.) Even though this is still a low number of individuals relative to the estimated 15,500 staff members at the nation's active grantmaking foundations, nonetheless, the group as a whole can be viewed as a microcosm representing large and small grantmakers and family, independent, community, and corporate foundations, those with primarily local programs and those whose reach is national and even international. For the sake of continuity, every effort was made to include interviewees from prior editions. Many, however, had moved on to other careers or retired.

The interviewees were highly enthusiastic, both about their participation in the compilation of this guide and about the prospects for philanthropy in general. As is evident, they had a lot to say about a variety of issues. They took the conversation very seriously, many having given our questions much prior thought and preparation. In nearly doubling the number of grantmakers we talked to, we made every effort to include as diverse a group as possible. Almost every grantmaker we approached to be interviewed for this book said "yes," a clear indication of one of the trends we'll remark on immediately: greatly increased interest on the part of grantmakers in making themselves accessible to the public. Those grantmakers we interviewed were extremely gracious, generous with their time, and, above all, interested in seeing grantseekers succeed in the future.

Overview

What aspects of the proposal review process are grantmakers focusing on today? What concerns them? What are the trends they see in the grantmaking and philanthropic worlds? Though we asked a series of wide-ranging questions, our interviewees' comments can be divided into three broad categories: the relationship with the nonprofit organization leading to a grant; the internal decision-making process of the grantmaker; and new trends in the wider philanthropic arena.

The grantmakers we interviewed tend to view the donor-donee relationship as highly personalized. They take a very hands-on approach to the nonprofits that seek their support, in many instances being proactively engaged in identifying potential grant recipients, rather than waiting to be asked. Early on in the submission process, they express themselves as more than willing to receive preliminary phone calls from grantseekers and to talk with them about their projects before any materials are sent out. However, they also caution grantseekers to think through their project goals very carefully before that phone call. It is critical at this delicate early stage not to waste a moment of the grantmaker's time. Grants decision makers are looking for a solid plan that is rooted in the agency's overall strategies for success and that demonstrates the organization's sustainability. "Sustainability," in fact, seems to be a "buzzword" for grantmakers in the new millennium.

As the process moves ahead and the prospective funder has demonstrated an interest, many grantmakers want to be involved in the actual proposal design. They also look favorably on evidence of collaboration among nonprofits as part of the proposal. They view various elements of responsible grant administration, such as reporting back on the grant and evaluation of outcomes, as mandatory. And they feel a responsibility to respond to calls seeking information regarding the next step, even in the case of rejection.

Every grantmaker we spoke to sees his or her foundation as unique. Each has a carefully conceived proposal review process. This may include interim calls or meetings with the nonprofit grantseeker and hard-won approvals at both staff and trustee levels. Those we interviewed agree that there is no "silver bullet" to speed the grantseeker through this process, just hard work. They take their work very seriously and expect the grantseeker to do so as well. To quote Joel Orosz of the W. K. Kellogg Foundation, "There is that important moment in the relationship when the program officer is no longer the gatekeeper but becomes your advocate." At this point, they may become passionate advocates indeed.

Our most dramatic finding from the series of interviews is that philanthropy is in the midst of a sea change. The grantmakers we talked to all mentioned the fact that this is the most dynamic period of growth for private philanthropy in recent decades. This growth is fueled by three related factors: the positive economy resulting in creation of wealth, the tremendous increase in family foundations, and the advent of venture philanthropy. The first factor makes the latter two possible. The interviewees note that the new family foundations are motivated to give but in need of guidance. They represent a great cultivation challenge for grantseekers. The verdict is still out on venture philanthropy. Some see it as a stimulus for change in grantmaking, others as a possible "flash in the pan." Still others fear that anything less than immediate success will cause some of these entrepreneurs to walk away from philanthropy. Virtually all of our interviewees agree that these trends are important issues for grantseekers to be aware of.

Technology

Since the prior edition of this guide, there have been enormous technological strides made in the grantmaking community. Very much unlike the last time we held such conversations, a mere four years ago, nearly every interviewee either has a Web site or is in the process of creating one. Most of the 39 grantmakers interviewed now communicate with applicants and grantees by e-mail, and many even say that e-mail is now their preferred mode of communication. Some of the grantmakers interviewed now accept a preliminary letter of inquiry in an online format. Many more are working toward that new procedure, with the initial step being e-mail. A few are accepting proposals electronically, and many more interviewees are actively exploring ways to make this happen. Some of the veteran grantmakers we interviewed, however, still openly admit a fondness for paper. They are frustrated by this transitional period when part of the application is electronic and parts (the attachments, for example) are still in hard copy format. They agree, however, that the next wave of program officers will be even more computer literate, and thus more comfortable with the electronic medium.

What You Will Find in This Chapter

For clarity's sake we have included the questions we posed to the thirty-nine interviewees and a selection of their responses. On some questions, there was remarkable agreement. For these we selected a half dozen or so representative comments. On other questions, there was greater difference of opinion. For those we chose responses that seem to indicate the various trains of thought, without being repetitive. Some of the comments not included here will be found throughout the rest of the text as quotes selected to exemplify key points being made.

Do you find that most grantseekers have done their homework (research) before contacting you?

Half do, half don't. Often newer organizations, or those that have never been funded, do not do their homework. (Peter Bird)

They do their homework and find that they do not fit, but they try anyway. They send mass mailers—these are a waste of postage. (Lynn Feldhouse)

We get many appeals that don't fit, about eight out of ten. A fair number will undertake a word search and our foundation will come up. But then they fail to go further into our description of what we mean by our priorities. (Michael Gilligan)

Fewer are coming to us who are outside of our guidelines. Grant-seekers are more sophisticated. (Ilene Mack)

For the most part, established organizations submit well-prepared proposals. They have researched our grants programs and know how we like to communicate. (Charles H. McTier)

The majority (80%) don't fit. They are not looking at our prior grant-ees. (Greg Norton)

This varies enormously among grantseekers. Some have it down to a science. The worst thing is when a grantseeker brings an irrelevant project to us. Nonprofits should do their homework. They should treat us like a partner. (Elizabeth Reveal)

Most have, but there are exceptions. Some come without a project. Some send cold applications without any idea what the foundation wants. A larger proportion have looked at our brochure and followed instructions. However, things are better now than ten years ago. (Charles Rooks)

Most grantseekers are doing their homework. Many talk to us even before sending a letter of inquiry. We hold information sessions monthly about our review process. (Beth Smith)

Sometimes, even if they have the resources to research potential funders, many grantseekers are off the mark; often they have assumptions about the grantmakers (or grantmaking) and filter the information through that perspective. (Ellen Wert)

What is the best initial approach to your foundation?

We have an open door policy. We will chat on the phone, communicate on the Web, whatever. This helps us to get to know the community, people, and needs. It is good to talk out an idea on the phone. This saves time for everyone. (Peter Bird)

We accept preliminary applications, via both e-mail and regular mail. (Ruby Lerner)

We are happy to speak with applicants [by telephone]. It is a mutual education process. (John Murphy)

Either a telephone call or full proposal draft is fine. (David Odahowski)

After the letter of inquiry, we may invite a proposal. The great majority of these go to the staff for review. (Joel Orosz)

First, we want to see a two-page letter of intent and financial information (project budget and organization budget). Then, we may or may not invite a proposal. (Julie Rogers)

The nonprofit should send a full proposal in order to have an adequate review by the trustees. Whenever we can, we will answer questions and see the nonprofit before the proposal is sent. (Charles Rooks)

We are accessible to answer questions over the phone. A letter of inquiry is a more formal way to determine if the agency or program meets our guidelines. That way, applicants won't waste their time or the foundation staff's time if a request is not appropriate. (Beth Smith)

Applicants for grants are asked to submit a letter that briefly describes the proposed area of work, the importance of the problem to be addressed, and the strategies to be employed. The letter should include an estimate of the total funds needed and the amount requested from the foundation, a proposed schedule and work plan, expected outcomes, and the relevant qualifications of the person or people who would direct the project. (Rik Treiber)

Assuming the nonprofit is within our guidelines, then it is okay to submit a proposal. (E. Belvin Williams)

How do you usually read a grant request?

I read the project section and the budget. I look at the board list to see how many people are on the board. If it is a new organization with too few board members, it may be too fragile to be funded. (Jessie Bond)

I look at everything. In particular I want to see other donors and who serves on the board of directors. Whether I read from beginning to end depends on how long the document is. (Hunter Corbin)

I read the project section and look for outcomes, approach, and capacity to implement. All elements of the proposal should interrelate. They should be consistent with the mission and strategies. (Susan Lajoie Eagan)

I look at the need section, the project section, and the timetable for implementation. (Cynthia Evans)

I often look at the budget and then read the proposal backwards. (Michael Gilligan)

I read the cover letter first, hoping it will contain a quick, concise statement of what the proposal says. Ideally, it should make me *want* to read the full proposal. (J. Andrew Lark)

I love to get a good executive summary, one that gives me the pertinent information, clearly written, in a concise write-up. (Ilene Mack)

First the need section, then the budget. The budget is a tool, not an end. I also read the project section to look for evidence of innovation and whether the agency is able to be a model so that others can replicate the project. (John Murphy)

I read the cover letter. It helps me quickly figure out what they are asking for. (Greg Norton)

I look at the budget. Over the years I've learned that narrative can be enriching, but the numbers are stark and straightforward. I want to see that the money is doing the job described in the proposal. (Joel Orosz)

I skip around the document in the following way: first the budget, to see if the request is appropriate and to see the agency's financials; then the project section, to see what they want to accomplish; then the board list. (Lynn Pattillo)

It depends on the organization. With bigger, older organizations I read the program content. I look at the budget, audit, and 990 for newer applicants. I also do a reasonableness check: employees/ volunteers vs. the number of kids served. (E. Belvin Williams)

We look for the relationship between the project section and the budget. (Kirke Wilson)

Does your foundation/corporation acknowledge in writing all proposals it receives?

No, but we are considering doing this. (Lynn Feldhouse)

Yes, this is usually done in writing or via telephone, depending on the time line. We also send e-mail. We communicate, especially if anything is missing from the application. (Michael Gilligan)

We respond by letter within forty-eight hours. (Charles H. McTier)

We respond to all inquiries and proposals. We review proposals and respond promptly, noting what is missing from the application. (David Odahowski)

Yes, in writing or electronically. (Joel Orosz)

No, there is too great a volume. (E. Belvin Williams)

How long does the process of review typically take at your foundation/corporation?

For unrestricted requests, two and a half months. (Jessie Bond)

Initial review takes one to one and a half months. (Hunter Corbin)

Four to six weeks on average. Online letters of inquiry are usually processed in one week. (Lynn Feldhouse)

We do initial screening expeditiously and notify grantseekers of the result. The time for a competitive grant to reach our board for final decision, however, varies by program area. It usually is not feasible to meet requests for immediate or near-term funding. (Jonathan T. Howe)

Three to six months unless we have a full agenda or the document is incomplete. (David Odahowski)

Two to four months. Ninety-eight percent of the proposals we receive are complete—they have all the attachments we need for review. (Charles Rooks)

Once a proposal is pending, is it okay for the grantseeker to call you to check on the status of the request or to share information? Is it okay to send additional materials?

Occasionally, grantseekers will communicate with us, usually by mail. They should be sure to tell us if the agency receives a major grant or if there are major changes in the organization. This could impact our decision. I would recommend that an organization not go overboard. (Jessie Bond)

We prefer them to do this in writing. We rarely visit, so a call is okay. We will let them know what is missing. If there is too much contact, we will say so. (Hunter Corbin)

It helps keep us up to date. It is a big problem if we do not hear about a major institutional change. It is important for us to know about other grants received for the project under consideration. (Roxanne Ford)

Additional materials are often helpful because the process leading to a grant can be lengthy. Things can change for the grantseeker, and we need to know that. (Heather Graham)

They should feel welcome to call to see how their request is progressing. We receive many requests, but it is easy for us to check if their request is logged into our system. We willingly accept updates of the information submitted and additional materials. (Reatha Clark King)

Usually a note or a call is a good idea, but not every day! The grant-maker should not be kept in the dark. If the organization has gotten a grant from another funder, we would love to hear about that as well—success is wonderful. We never make you feel like a suppli-cant. We will give honest input. However, we also want to hear any negative news from the grantee, rather than from an outside source. (Ilene Mack)

There is a fine line between informing and lobbying. (John Murphy)

Absolutely! It is good to communicate on a regular basis. Tell your story over and over. Do it well and respectfully; recount success sto-ries. (David Odahowski)

I really want to know what's going on. This might make me more interested. It is important to give me new information—a heads up. Remember at some point the program officer switches from being a gatekeeper to being an advocate. That is when additional informa-tion is especially appreciated. (Joel Orosz)

We prefer to talk to the person on the front line about the specifics of the program, not the development officer. A good development offi-cer should see him/herself as part of the team and a problem solver. It is fine if the grantseeker calls once to touch base: Did you receive the packet? Do you have any questions? Is there anything else you need? (Lynn Pattillo)

If we never hear anything, that is not a good sign. (Jane Polin)

If there is anything significant that has happened, or if the applicant has received other support, this can be very important. The non-profit has the responsibility to get additional material and informa-tion to us. We also encourage grantees to come to us, even when they are having problems. (Beth Smith)

It may take four to six weeks to review a project. If the four to six weeks has passed, and the grantseeker hasn't been notified of a deci-sion . . . they are encouraged to call back a couple of weeks later to check on the status. However, the foundation strongly prefers to pro-vide grant decisions in writing. Grantseekers are always welcome to submit additional information, and that information is simply added to the proposal packet. (Rik Treiber)

Is it all right if a board member from the applying organization contacts one of your board members directly?

This is a great way to antagonize foundation staff. The staff knows the board very well. We know what they will like and not like. There is trust between our staff and board. Most times, the board members will tell the grantseeker to go to the staff. In placing the request, let the process take its course. (Peter Bird)

We don't mind, as long as they don't push too hard. (Hunter Corbin)

People do contact our trustees. When they do, they are told to send something to the staff. It is our policy that the first contact be with staff. (Kay Dusenbery)

Handling grantseekers is a staff job. We need to follow procedures. We question the motives of an organization that will go to the board. The board does not appreciate being lobbied. It puts the board in an unfair position. (Lynn Feldhouse)

We have to allow this. There is no way to stop it. The decision, however, is based on merit. (David Ford)

We prefer that applicants work through staff, but you can't control who is going to talk to whom. Certainly, if a trustee indicates a strong interest in a qualified proposal, we will factor that into the review. If contact is going to happen, I appreciate a "heads up." Then I am prepared for questions or comments from the trustees. (Roxanne Ford)

Our process is very clear and very open. There is no advantage in talking to individual trustees. They will not influence the process. Of course, it is not a disadvantage either if a trustee says he or she has heard of your nonprofit and lets it go at that. (Jonathan T. Howe)

This is often done. Keep in mind that we have a conflict of interest policy for board members, so the board will not lobby on behalf of an organization. (David Odahowski)

Go with the strong relationship but be conscientious and let the staff know. (Jane Polin)

Do you expect reports/evaluations from grantees? Do you remind a grantee when you expect the evalution(s)/reports to be submitted?

We ask applicants to project the outcomes of the program in the application. In the letter to the nonprofit announcing the grant, we list these project outcomes as a reminder. We include a list of questions we want the grantee to use as the base of the report. It also indicates the dates reports are due to us. If the report is late, we send a reminder letter. (Jessie Bond)

We always ask for an assessment section in the proposal. Grant-seekers need training in how to assess the success of the project. They need to gather models of approaches and tools. We have information on our Web site for grantees to work with. We also have workshops to help them learn more about assessment practices. (Cynthia Evans)

We don't want reports to be burdensome. We want an anecdotal report in one year detailing how the money was spent, according to the budget, and that the project was successfully completed. We use this to analyze future grants. (Lynn Feldhouse)

We like to see plans for the evaluation in the proposal. We will communicate in writing and verbally what we expect by way of evaluation. (Jonathan T. Howe)

The evaluation section of the proposal should detail benchmarks in pursuing the project and how they will be reported. We have a suggested outline for progress reports which are due at the six- and twelve-month marks. We want to know how things are proceeding. We want the good and bad news. If the news is bad, we may be able to help. (J. Andrew Lark)

The extent of reporting depends on the nature of the project. We want to see something in the proposal about anticipated outcomes, broader impact, and assessment. We have an evaluation department, and we are working on a reporting form. This is an evolving process for us, but we will continue to work with grantees on it. (Penelope McPhee)

The award letter spells out our requirements. The complexity varies. It ranges from quarterly to annual reports. We do a final evaluation. Also, we do a hands-on technical assistance workshop for many grantees where they can share successes with one another. (John Murphy)

We are up front with grantees on the importance of reports. A summative evaluation is good. It tells us about the impact of the project. We want to know how you are doing. We will provide technical assistance to help formulate evaluations. (Joel Orosz)

We ask for evaluation parameters in the proposal. They do not have to be overly detailed. The letter indicating the grant tells about our reporting requirements. We conduct a site visit upon completion of the final report to give us a better idea of how things went. (David Palenchar)

Evaluation plans are generally weak in the proposal stage. But we assume that if an organization can visualize the project, they can report on its implementation. Reporting requirements are stated in our grant award letter. We require annual reports that include narrative and financial information. The report should reflect what happened and indicate whether the plans changed. We don't have to hear from the grantee every week. (Elspeth Revere)

We are investors in organizations. We expect to see reports that help us assess how an organization is doing. When we make a grant, this is a decision among competing interests. Reports help us assess our giving ability. (Hildy Simmons)

Following the rejection of an application, do you speak with the applicant about the declination if they ask you to?

I will pull the applicant's file and review with them why the proposal was declined. Often it is a lack of funds on our part. (Hunter Corbin)

We are happy to have a conversation about a rejection. The grant-seeker needs to gain an understanding about why they were turned down. (Kay Dusenbery)

Absolutely. This is important feedback. We will be very honest. (Roxanne Ford)

There is an amazing drop-off rate when an initial grant submission gets rejected. We seldom ever hear from the agency again. If the request was outside our guidelines, we tell them. If the project is promising, we ask to be kept apprised. (J. Andrew Lark)

You have a right to an explanation. There are a wide variety of responses from grantmakers: some say "please don't call." Others liken the rejection to breaking up a romance: they don't want to rehash it. I dread an emotional conversation or when the person is angry. When I have been an advocate for a project and pushed to get it funded but we still say no, I feel bad too. (Joel Orosz)

The rejection letter may contain feedback. We try to address each applicant personally. This is tricky. A grant request is not like a term paper, right or wrong. We don't say that it is a lousy proposal. We advise applicants to wait one year before submitting another request. (David Palenchar)

I often speak to grantseekers. I also send notes and give feedback in writing. Grantmakers spend the bulk of their time saying no, but should encourage the grantseeker to seek support elsewhere. Often if they were declined here, it was because the request was not a fit. (Jane Polin)

The grantmaker has to be willing to communicate at this point. (Elizabeth Reveal)

I am happy to have this conversation if someone from the organization calls. This almost never happens; I am impressed when it does. (Elspeth Revere)

A conversation like this can be hard and often unsatisfying. Sometimes there really isn't anything to say because the proposal may have been very good, but it did not meet the interests of our trustees. We try to point out how the application could have been stronger. We have these conversations only when we seriously review a request, not following an early declination. (Charles Rooks)

Following the rejection of an application, what is the best thing an organization can do?

There are three things a grantseeker should do. Say thank you, profusely, for considering the request. Tell the grantmaker how you will pursue support from here. Keep cultivating us. (Peter Bird)

Say thank you, especially if we all worked cooperatively. (David Ford)

Give us at the foundation honest feedback about our process and behavior—though I appreciate that this is often hard for a grantseeker to do. (Heather Graham)

Recognize that being turned down is not a permanent rejection. Come back again. Don't give up. There is a lot of competition and not enough money. (Jonathan T. Howe)

Realize that a turndown is never personal. Step back and be objective. If you have questions, feel free to call us. The declination may not be forever. (Ilene Mack)

Do more research on other possible funding sources. Be resilient and persistent. (Charles H. McTier)

Follow up and ascertain why. Get feedback. Build a relationship with us and open the channels of communication. (Julie Rogers)

Being disappointed is very understandable, but an applicant should understand that we have to make difficult choices and that a rejection is not personal. (Beth Smith)

Send a letter asking if you can reapply. We turn applications down for two reasons. Either we ran out of grant money or the agency or their project was not a high priority for us. (E. Belvin Williams)

Following the rejection of an application, what is the worst thing an organization can do?

Show frustration and anger. There may be opportunities in the future for support, and you don't want to alienate everyone at the foundation. (Kay Dusenbery)

Have a hostile reaction, write to my board chair or come to see the CEO. This elevates the tension level and prevents productive dialogue. (Susan Lajoie Eagan)

Keep coming back, when you know you are not a match. (Cynthia Evans)

Complain to the board or inside leaders. This is a waste of time and doesn't work. (David Ford)

Not take "no" for an answer. The staff and board devote an enormous amount of time to making these decisions. We hope the applicant will respect that. (Roxanne Ford)

Send the same proposal in for our next meeting. This is a waste of time and energy. (A. Thomas Hildebrandt)

Give up and feel it is hopeless, or feel outraged. Often a request is rejected not because of worthiness but due to timing and priorities. (John E. Marshall III)

"Bad mouth" the process and say that the foundation is unfair. (John Murphy)

The worst thing is for a representative of a nonprofit organization to be angry, but not talk to us about it. Instead he or she tells everyone else in the community, and it gets back to us indirectly. (David Odahowski)

If a grant is awarded, what is the best thing an organization can do?

Go to work and do what you said you would do. Keep open channels of communication. (Kay Dusenbery)

Do fine work. Serve the kids well. Give us a concise flavor of what is happening. (David Ford)

Be a success beyond expectation. Send in the required reports. This provides good feedback. (Jonathan T. Howe)

Apply time and energy to making the project succeed. Be dedicated to making a difference. (Reatha Clark King)

Get on with the work and do a good job. Let us know how things are progressing. Be honest with us about what's happening. We realize that things can change over the course of time. (Penelope McPhee)

Make communication easily digestible. Tell us success stories, give us reports, be honest and straightforward. (Elizabeth Reveal)

Keep us informed about what the organization is doing. We look at correspondence and newsletters. If there is a change in a grantee's leadership, funders need to hear about it. We also like to hear good news. Invite us to annual meetings, special events. We do try to go. (Beth Smith)

If a grant is awarded, what is the worst thing an organization can do?

Take the money and run, then communicate nothing about what's going on. It is always a disappointment when we only hear from them when they need money. They should think about the funder as part of their organization and keep the funder informed. (Peter Bird)

Spend the money on something other than the purpose for which it was approved. (Jessie Bond)

Not say thank you. Run into trouble and fail to share it with us. You should fax or call—something—to keep us informed. (Lynn Feldhouse)

Neglect reporting or send inadequate reports. Not doing what you said you would do. (Roxanne Ford)

Use funds fraudulently. Misuse the funds without telling us. This makes a bad relationship. (Reatha Clark King)

Issue a press release without foundation approval. There are a lot of instances where the wrong interpretation can be applied as to why a grant was awarded. And obviously, misusing the money is always a no-no. (Ilene Mack)

Not being honest. Failure to follow up and keep on track with their commitment to us. If we pick up the newspaper and find the grantee fired its director, this damages its long-term reputation. (John Murphy)

Not acknowledge our letter. Not tell us bad news early on. If there is a problem, there is a lot we can do to help. (David Odahowski)

Act disappointed and/or be critical about the amount of the grant. (Charles Rooks)

Overwhelm us with information. This is not a good use of time and resources. (Hildy Simmons)

Beyond the basic information, should the proposal's cover letter contain any other data?

With automated phone services, it is impossible to reach people. Tell me the extension number so I can get through easily. (Hunter Corbin)

Give us the name of your fiscal agent, if involved, and how the fiscal relationship will work. (Cynthia Evans)

I read the cover letter to see if this project is an institutional priority. (Michael Gilligan)

Reference to past grants we may have awarded to your nonprofit is helpful; new staff here may not be aware of all prior relationships. (Heather Graham)

Often I can't find the amount of the request up front. Also, if the letter is signed by the top executive, give us a direct dial number for the development person. (Ilene Mack)

Reference to a prior conversation or grant is very important. Make us aware of any history with our foundation. We get frustrated when this is not clear and up front. (Joel Orosz)

Set the context: how do I know this agency—remind me. Indicate the next step and who will take it. Let us know how to reach you. (Jane Polin)

Be careful to be very accurate about prior meetings and discussions. (Charles Rooks)

The letter should be on the nonprofit's letterhead. Include the start and end dates of the project, also tell us the contact person and fiscal agent. (Ruth Shack)

Who should sign the cover letter?

Since we work with the CEO, we expect that is who will sign the letter. The development officer should sign in a few, rare cases. (Peter Bird)

The CEO should sign the cover letter. However, some cover letters are signed by development people. (Kay Dusenbery)

A signature of an officer or delegate of the board usually indicates that the board endorses the proposal. More importantly, though, the letter must be on the letterhead of the legal entity applying for the grant, such as the sponsor, if there is one. (Heather Graham)

We insist that the CEO sign the cover letter. This shows that the request is a priority of the institution and that it has gone through internal vetting. It shows that it is the highest priority of the institution's leadership. (Jonathan T. Howe)

This is not an issue for us. (Greg Norton)

It is better when the letter has been signed by the CEO. Make sure that the foundation's name is spelled correctly and that the address is right. The grantseeker's credibility is damaged before the envelope is opened if the foundation's name is not spelled correctly. (Lynn Pattillo)

Beyond the basic information, should the proposal contain any other data?

Timeline. Five-year business plan, if one exists. The nonprofit should show that it has a plan to become self-supporting in the future. (Kay Dusenbery)

This is a people business. We need to get a sense of the people behind the application. We want to know that there are dedicated volunteers working to transform the organization. (John E. Marshall III)

The budget should reflect the plan and how resources will be allocated to implement it. (Jane Polin)

A table of contents. (Elspeth Revere)

Don't assume that we know too much. Some agencies don't tell us enough about their field. A poorly written proposal fails to capture the foundation's attention. Invest time to flesh it out to produce something compelling. (Charles Rooks)

Include population served, and the number of staff and volunteers. (Ruth Shack)

The foundation asks for a full project budget as well as a budget showing the proposed use of funds, if other sources of funding are expected. In addition, CVs of key project staff, a timeline, and anticipated outcomes are all considered in funding decisions. (Rik Treiber)

Sustainability of the project/agency. Also, risk assessment: board, finances, leadership. Be short and concise. (Eugene R. Wilson)

You need to remember that you are in the "idea business." You have to use the document to get across your project. (Kirke Wilson)

Beyond the basic information, should the appendix contain any other data?

Letters from collaborative partners. These show that the partners are committed. (Jessie Bond)

Resumes of key people. (Cynthia Evans)

Strategic or long-range plan. (Michael Gilligan)

List of foundation/corporate donors to the project. We do not want to be the sole supporter of a project. (A. Thomas Hildebrandt)

Licenses and accreditation, if any. (John E. Marshall III)

What are the other sources of funds for the project? We need to know the agency is ready to move forward, and available life lines. (John Murphy)

A document from the board authorizing the request. This shows that the board is in sync with the fundraising effort. (David Palenchar)

Diversity analysis of board and staff. (Kirke Wilson)

As proposal attachments, do you find brochures, videos, newspaper clippings, anecdotal information, and endorsements useful?

These attachments do have a value. They add information about the nonprofit. But send a limited amount. Support letters are extraneous. (Jessie Bond)

On the whole, these materials will not be read. If you have to send something extra, mark clearly what you want us to look at. (Hunter Corbin)

I would ask that nonprofits be judicious in their choice of extra materials that they send. These really do not factor into our decision making. (Kay Dusenbery)

Too much information can be a real disincentive. If you are unsure about whether to send something, call the funder and ask. (Susan Lajoie Eagan)

Send in a limited amount and only if they are key and should be seen. Don't inundate us. (Cynthia Evans)

Initially, we don't want to see any of this. We hate to see an organization waste its efforts with all of this, only to find that they or their project does not fall within our guidelines. Once we have established a relationship, it is a different matter. (Heather Graham)

We don't need to use a lot of this. Use it as a cultivation tool. We do not look at it during our proposal review. (J. Andrew Lark)

Don't go to the expense of sending the grantmaker unessential information and materials. (Charles H. McTier)

Some of these materials can be helpful. They provide the human dimension. They give the proposal depth. (John Murphy)

I can see the organizational life cycle in an organization's materials. (David Odahowski)

Please don't overwhelm us with too much material. Do you know that with one application, I got the last twelve issues of the agency's newsletter plus a photo of the board chair! (Hildy Simmons)

If the agency is new to the foundation, these can be okay. Otherwise, it is a waste of paper and can be overwhelming. Don't send resumes if they are not asked for. (Beth Smith)

Some supplemental information is good but a huge quantity is not necessary. (Eugene R. Wilson)

Can you share any specific feedback about the physical presentation of a proposal?

Use an easy-to-read font. Use binder clips. Do not bind the proposal. (Hunter Corbin)

There is no hard and fast rule. Use your best judgment. (Kay Dusenbery)

Make it as easy as possible for the reader to get to the key information. I appreciate a table of contents. Don't use jargon; this is a turn off. Can the reasonably informed reader understand? The document has to be easily duplicated. (Susan Lajoie Eagan)

We discard covers. Jazzy doesn't help. We like reader-friendly text. (Michael Gilligan)

Break up a dense page. Binders or folders are not necessary. We take them off and put the proposal in our own file folders. Attachments should be clipped separately. (Heather Graham)

Generous spacing is helpful to the reader. We prefer that it not be bound. We prefer that the proposal not have a cover. Simple is better. Be sure it is accurate. (Jonathan T. Howe)

Gloss equals waste. (J. Andrew Lark)

Content is more important than form. Honesty is the best policy. Use clarity, no jargon. It should not be fancy; no binders, no tabs. (Ilene Mack)

More is not necessarily better. Our staff has to summarize the request for the board. The board sees the summary, not the full application. So it's in the applicant's best interest to state the case briefly and clearly. The applicant should be able to summarize it better than we can. (Penelope McPhee)

Generous margins. We write all over it! We like to see a proposal neat and professional, but not like a finished book. (Joel Orosz)

If the articulation is poor or the document is not put together in a way that it is easy to find things, then the proposal may get less favorable attention. We can't spend time trying to eke out the ideas. (Charles Rooks)

If it looks sloppy, it sends a signal. Don't make it overly fancy; no binders, no color. (Eugene R. Wilson)

Does your foundation/corporation have a Web site?

The majority of grantmakers interviewed indicated that they have a Web site.

We are more interactive than we thought we would be. We are regularly referring people to our Web site for updated information. (Cynthia Evans)

On our Web site we update grants awarded quarterly. We also update our guidelines. Eventually, we may not put grants and guidelines information in our other publications but only on the Web page. (Michael Gilligan)

Not yet. We are a local grantmaker. We generally do not fund groups located far outside of our geographic region. (J. Andrew Lark)

This is a huge change. Agencies can get information without intermediaries. (Elizabeth Reveal)

Our 990 and annual report are on our Web site. The Web site provides accessibility. It helps us maintain our accountability. Grantseekers can learn a great deal about us through our Web site. (Eugene R. Wilson)

Do you use e-mail to communicate with grantseekers?

The majority indicate that they do use e-mail.

This is our preferred mode of communication when we need additional information on a request. (Peter Bird)

We are testing ideas on e-mail. This is great. Agencies respond quickly. (David Ford)

I love it! It is easy to reach people. There is no problem about the time difference. You get a fast response. (Roxanne Ford)

We use e-mail to communicate during the middle period, while developing the proposal. This allows information to move faster and is more precise than the telephone. After a grant is awarded, there is a lot of contact via e-mail. (Michael Gilligan)

There is little communication via e-mail. Most people communicate personally. (A. Thomas Hildebrandt)

We use a variety of techniques, including e-mail. Our grantseekers also use a variety of techniques including telephone, e-mail, voice mail, and fax. Our foundation expects to use e-mail much more in the future. (Reatha Clark King)

When the nonprofit initiates it, we will use e-mail. A lot of our communication is by fax. (Charles H. McTier)

This is a double-edged sword. It is great for reference and research and for fast distribution, also for interim communication. On the other hand, we all receive too many e-mail messages each day. (Jane Polin)

Via e-mail, we reach geographical areas that are hard to reach in other ways. We reach organizations in a non-hierarchical manner. (Elizabeth Reveal)

We are starting to communicate with grantseekers via e-mail. It is just a matter of time. We will do more with it. It depends on the style of the program officer. (Julie Rogers)

The foundation accepts letters of inquiry and proposal materials by e-mail, and occasional notifications of declined proposals are provided via e-mail, particularly for letters or proposals submitted electronically. Foundation staff work with prospective grantees to develop projects, and much of this communication is handled via e-mail. (Rik Treiber)

We often use e-mail during the grant period. But during the review process, we communicate face-to-face or by phone. (Ellen Wert)

Whatever works for the nonprofit. (Kirke Wilson)

Does your foundation/corporation accept proposals electronically?

We have two RFP projects that we handle via e-mail. Straightforward applications lend themselves well to electronic media. We do not yet accept more general proposals electronically. Right now, we're redesigning our Web site to allow organizations to create and save an application, even coming back to it before final submission. We think this is where things are headed electronically. (Peter Bird)

For the near term, applications will not be accepted online. We need to put a system in place to track their receipt. (Jessie Bond)

We need the right medium to do this. The hard copy proposal lets me see how the organization communicates. (Hunter Corbin)

Yes, but not many organizations do this. When we receive e-mailed documents, there is frequently a formatting problem. Since we are a local foundation, a lot of the nonprofits we fund are located quite close by. They bring the proposal to the foundation's office. (Kay Dusenbery)

In a few years we will. Our world is heading in the direction of grantees' increased use of technology. We are not quite there yet. Community foundations need to be accessible to different nonprofits that may not be technologically savvy. (Susan Lajoie Eagan)

We are concerned about the digital divide. Fiscal materials are sent separately. (David Ford)

I don't see this happening. I wish we could be more flexible about this, but not all nonprofits have computer technology. This is a reading-intensive business. An advantage to the applicant is that if the nonprofit prepares the proposal, they have control over how the packet looks. (Roxanne Ford)

I am eager for the day we have a good database of e-mail information for our donees and grantseekers. Grantseekers will get much better customer service as we increase the use of electronic tools. (Reatha Clark King)

I need to have it on paper. I highlight when I read. Speed is not always of the essence. (Ilene Mack)

This has gone very well. It helps to streamline the process. If the proposal is submitted online, we get the other information via mail. (Greg Norton)

It will not happen overnight. There is a generation of foundation leaders who are not comfortable with technology. The written document has more impact now. (David Odahowski)

We have a pre-application form. We originally had a lot of trepidation about this. We didn't want to force applicants into a cookie cutter and lose the energy of their ideas. Submitting the proposal via e-mail is now possible. (Joel Orosz)

We have talked about this but have not gotten to that point yet. Since we ask for photos and financials, electronic transmission is unwieldy. (David Palenchar)

This is an experiment. We accept a letter of intent on e-mail. We want to help grantees with technology. We are at the forefront of technology in the region. It is our job to push and lead. (Julie Rogers)

We require things they can't send electronically, such as audits, etc. We don't want the burden of having to piece things together. (Charles Rooks)

The information that we need is hard to get electronically. My style of work is that I like to sit back in a chair and read the materials. I like to make notes and underline. I like to see the texture of the proposal document. (Hildy Simmons)

We need to have the proposal on letterhead, in hard copy. (Ellen Wert)

Are there things you wish grantseekers would do better?

The single biggest mistake is when a grantseeker asks for a huge amount of money because there is a need. They ignore the typical size grants and interests of the grantmaker. (Peter Bird)

People looking for grants need to understand that need is not enough. Theirs is not the only issue that should be funded. An organization must have the capacity to do what they say they are going to do. (Jessie Bond)

It is very frustrating when we can't get a feel for an organization or what they are asking us for from the proposal. Often in a poor proposal there are a lot of buzzwords and jargon. (Hunter Corbin)

When an organization requests two to three times more money than we initially discussed, it doesn't sit well with the foundation staff. We strongly prefer no surprises in the process. (Kay Dusenbery)

I am frustrated when the grantseeker does not send the proposal to the correct address or does not send the correct number of copies. (Lynn Feldhouse)

Grantseekers need to be concise. They need to improve on the quality of writing. (David Ford)

Grantseekers first should review the grantmaker's written guidelines, if these are available. Many nonprofits fail to understand the process grantseekers should follow and the issues grantmakers face in providing good service. (Reatha Clark King)

Get the application in early! Don't work against such a tight schedule. (J. Andrew Lark)

Tell the program officer when he/she has done something wrong. I get so little constructive feedback. No one has the courage, and for good reason: there is a significant power imbalance. (Joel Orosz)

People who have not done appropriate project design are a frustration. You have to do your planning up front. (Elizabeth Reveal)

When I am out and about in the community, it's hard to be solicited all the time. I like to just talk socially and am happy to receive a business call at the office. (Julie Rogers)

My frustration is with the nonprofit that sends me six proposals and asks which one I want. (Kirke Wilson)

Would you share a specific tip or two?

When you write, don't assume that the donor knows anything. We are not experts in the nonprofit's field. Do research. Know what the grantmaker will and will not do. (Hunter Corbin)

Meet deadlines. Honor our requests for information and respond on time. This tells us that the organization is efficient and that their request to us is important to them. (Kay Dusenbery)

Try to have a conversation with the grantmaker, either on the phone or in person. This can help the relationship. Research, research, research; see what prior grants went for. (David Ford)

Listen to what we tell you so you will know what the next step is. It is hard to wear out your welcome if you listen. (Roxanne Ford)

Get many eyes on a proposal as it is being developed. Project the institutional view, not the personal view. (Michael Gilligan)

Don't contact us only when you want money. (A. Thomas Hildebrandt)

Don't be hesitant to call and ask. Assume you are welcome to call and inquire. Be optimistic. Good communication requires patience; it is a journey traveled together. Think through the brilliance of your idea and how it relates to the problems you are addressing. (Reatha Clark King)

Ask who else to go to for funding. Grantseekers rarely ask this but we often times help, especially when we have funded them and have a vested interest. (J. Andrew Lark)

Communicate your passion. People will be excited by what you are doing. (Ruby Lerner)

Listen for the "no." Be professional. Don't take turndowns personally and stop listening. Be careful while you persist in calling for information. Don't cross the border into pestering. (Ilene Mack)

Honesty. We are all in this business because we are convinced that nonprofits do wonderful work. We are all on the same side. It is not productive to try to pull the wool over our eyes. (Penelope McPhee)

1. Be committed.
2. Be capable.
3. Be honest.
4. Be concise.
5. Be accountable.
6. Be trustworthy.

(Charles H. McTier)

Don't limit your horizon. Use the grantmaker's help to stretch. (John Murphy)

A challenge to the grantseeker is knowing where the grantmaker is on the continuum. Is their approach formal or informal? (Jane Polin)

Cultivate the relationship with a grantmaker over time. As the players change, get to know the new program people. (Julie Rogers)

Listen carefully instead of hearing what you want to hear. (Charles Rooks)

Don't give up. Come back. It is not easy raising money, but having a proposal rejected once does not mean that an agency will be rejected in the future. (Beth Smith)

Ask questions at every opportunity. Say what you need. We want to be helpful. If we don't award a grant, we can steer you in the right direction. (Ellen Wert)

Have you noticed new trends in grantmaking today?

Grantmakers are asking for accountability. Collaborative efforts are a big plus. I am impressed with the organization that can demonstrate its success. (Peter Bird)

There is more evaluation. For community foundations, there is more of an effort to connect discretionary and donor-advised funds. (Jessie Bond)

The Internet can be used to obtain information on grantmakers and grantseekers. It is an important vehicle. (Kay Dusenbery)

There is growing concern and interest in organizational capacity. We are seeing more requests for human resources, fundraising, handheld computers, and technological capacity tied to service delivery. (Susan Lajoie Eagan)

Grantmakers are proactive in seeking out nonprofits. They are making multi-year grants that are for flexible core operating support. In ten years all communications will be electronic. (Cynthia Evans)

The number of requests received from outside the United States is exploding. This is putting a strain on the system. We are hearing from groups that we have never heard from in the past. The groups are smaller and are government funded. We are seeing professionally produced proposals. The quality is going up. The sheer volume is up: 50% in just the last year. (Lynn Feldhouse)

We are seeing more grants that feature collaborations either with institutions or between different institutions. We believe this approach has a lot of merit and have made several such grants recently. (Roxanne Ford)

Support for planning. Grantmakers are making fewer and larger grants. Grantmakers are working more closely with grantees, fostering and supporting efforts that increase effective organizational management and assessment. (Heather Graham)

There are many more smaller and less sophisticated organizations applying to us for grants. Serving them well takes patience on our part. We hope to see more of this trend. I think we have stimulated it, and we are delighted to have these organizations participate. (Reatha Clark King)

There is a blurring of the lines between government responsibility and what foundations do, especially in the area of education. (J. Andrew Lark)

Outcome, accountability, impact: more and more today there is an increasing understanding of what is a good investment. Also, sustainability is an issue: funders want to know that you will be better off at the end of the grant period than you were at the beginning. (Ruby Lerner)

Nonprofits are better at what they do, including their business and fundraising. More people have the correct understanding about what philanthropy is. There is more collaboration between agencies and foundations. Nonprofits realize that they can't rely on one source of income. They must have a diversified funding base. (Ilene Mack)

It will be interesting to see how venture philanthropy shakes out and if it has any impact on regular foundation, corporate, and individual giving. It is a different paradigm. (John E. Marshall, III)

Technical assistance for capacity building is being awarded in addition to money. Grantmakers want to provide help in other ways than giving money. (Penelope McPhee)

We are in an unparalleled economic boom. Enormous wealth has been created. There are more donors who are giving very large grants. But I am concerned about some of this new giving. Many new donors don't understand the broad needs in their community in the same way that traditional philanthropy does. I am concerned that they may not stick around. (Charles H. McTier)

Partnerships: grantmakers view grantees as partners, sort of an extended family. Funders are collaborating because they want to use their limited funds strategically. Grantmakers are coaching and encouraging nonprofits to stretch. (John Murphy)

Capacity building: infrastructure, management. Social entrepreneurship. The creation of wealth. (David Odahowski)

There is a huge wave of money coming at us—an intergenerational "transfer of wealth." Small organizations have a tremendous opportunity to go to foundations that didn't exist before. Research is the challenge. (Joel Orosz)

Some grantmakers are trying to make more grants; therefore grants are smaller in size. Grantmakers are moving away from larger nonprofits because of the size of a grant needed to have any real impact. They want to use their dollars where they will have the most impact. (David Palenchar)

This is an exciting moment in philanthropy. There is a new level of sophistication around public-private partnerships working together with their expertise and resources. This was not the case ten years ago. (Jane Polin)

There is a trend (that has been going on for a long time) toward project support, rather than general operating support. We need to be aware of this. Although it may not be as interesting for foundation staff to work on operating support grants, general support is important to nonprofits. (Elspeth Revere)

Outcome-based evaluation is an important movement. There are many new givers, and the ability to partner with them is exciting. (Julie Rogers)

Nonprofits are better managed. There are younger philanthropists who are idealistic but are naive and have unrealistic expectations. I hope they won't get turned off to philanthropy. They need to stick it out through disappointments. (Charles Rooks)

Grantmakers are receptive to multi-year grants, pushing time horizons. This is good, but often they don't know how much they have to give away in the future. (Hildy Simmons)

Funders are more focused, but they also have more money to give away. There are new foundations and other funders, including venture capitalists. This can be challenging to nonprofits because these funders may not communicate publicly about what they are interested in funding. But this will become clearer with time. (Beth Smith)

Many grantmakers are working hard to develop close relationships with their local nonprofits. Have you hugged a 501(c)(3) today? (Eugene R. Wilson)

There has been a dramatic growth in family philanthropy. They have more money than they ever imagined, and they want to do the right thing with it. There's also a sense of stewardship. Community foundations have changed character; they are community problem solvers and multi-dimensional, not just grantmakers. (Kirke Wilson)

Appendix A

Sample Proposal

October 31, 2000

Dear _____

Thank you for taking the time to speak with me on the phone yesterday and for providing Claremont Neighborhood Centers with an opportunity to submit a proposal to the Early Riser Fund. In Claremont's South Bronx community, young people ages 16–24 who are unemployed and not attending school are at great risk. Claremont's Project AJPHA (Acquiring Jobs to Promote Higher Aspirations) targets this difficult-to-reach group and offers the counseling and support that gets young people off the streets and into productive employment, vocational training and continuing education. Since last year, when Claremont began Project AJPHA, enrollment has more than doubled from 30 to 75, and we now maintain a waiting list of 45.

To help Claremont expand and enhance Project AJPHA to meet the needs of youth from our South Bronx community, we are requesting a grant of $25,000 from the Early Riser Fund. The support of the Early Riser Fund will allow Claremont to add staff and activities that motivate young people to choose a path that leads to success.

Enclosed please find a full proposal, as well as documents supporting the request. Please feel free to call me with any questions about Claremont, or Project AJPHA, or to arrange a visit.

We appreciate your consideration of this request.

Sincerely,

Rachel E. Spivey
Executive Director

Claremont Neighborhood Centers, Inc.
Project AJPHA:
Acquiring Jobs to Promote Higher Aspirations

A Proposal to:
Early Riser Fund

Submitted By:

Rachel Spivey, Executive Director
Claremont Neighborhood Centers, Inc.

489 East 169th Street
Bronx, New York 10456
(718) 588-1000

TABLE OF CONTENTS

EXECUTIVE SUMMARY

Since 1956, Claremont Neighborhood Centers, Inc. has worked to improve the quality of life for South Bronx residents by providing an array of services that build self-reliance and foster personal, educational, and professional achievement. Through Project AJPHA (Acquiring Jobs to Promote Higher Aspirations) Claremont provides employment readiness training, preparation, and referrals for out-of-school and unemployed youth ages 16–24 who are at risk of becoming lost to the streets.

Project AJPHA staff assess each young person's preemployment and educational needs and offer supportive services that open doors to employment and/or further education. After completing the program, participants have entered into full-time jobs, returned to high school, worked toward obtaining their GED, or enrolled in technical job training programs.

As young people from our neighborhood come to recognize that to find employment they must have marketable skills, the demand for Project AJPHA's services increases. In its first year, Project AJPHA served approximately 30 young people. Currently, the Project has an enrollment of 75 and maintains a waiting list of 45.

Claremont is seeking funds to enrich Project AJPHA's offerings and to better serve the young people in our community. Specifically, additional support will help enable Claremont to provide comprehensive job readiness programming that includes:

Increased program enrollment

An expanded computer training component

More internship opportunities at area corporations

Enhanced follow-up counseling and support for
    program graduates

Improved evaluation and tracking of program results

Claremont is requesting a grant of $25,000 from the Early Riser Fund to assist in the implementation of these enhancements to Project AJPHA. The support of the Early Riser Fund will be instrumental in helping Claremont build a base of financial support to ensure the Project's ongoing success in serving young people from the South Bronx.

STATEMENT OF NEED AND POPULATION SERVED

Due to the shrinking pool of unskilled entry-level job openings, as well the growing sophistication and knowledge required by today's labor market, it has become increasingly important for our young people to have assistance in their efforts to find long-term stable employment. The young adults from our neighborhood have often received insufficient support at school or at home to prepare them for gainful employment. The unemployment rate in the neighborhood is 65%. Approximately 40% of area residents never completed high school.

Claremont is located within a school district that has the highest absentee rate and the second lowest reading and math scores in the city. The two high schools that serve young people from our community have among the city's highest rates of overcrowding and drop-out.

Claremont designed Project AJPHA to serve one of the most vulnerable, yet difficult to reach groups in our community: youth ages 16–24 who are not attending school, not employed and not enrolled in any training or supportive program. Many of these young people lack role models who have stable employment experience, and most do not have the basic skills needed to find a job. The longer these young people are out of school and unemployed, the greater their risk of succumbing to criminal activity, substance abuse, and the persistent dangers associated with poverty. By providing assistance to these young people, Claremont not only improves their prospects for individual achievement, but also helps to contribute to the long-term stability and safety of our community.

GOALS OF PROJECT AJPHA

Claremont Neighborhood Centers, Inc.'s overall goal is to equip each of Project AJPHA's participants with the confidence and knowledge that will lead to a life of employment and self-sufficiency. Specific goals are to:

- Prepare applicants for the job search and interview process
- Provide opportunities for real world experience in work situations

- Offer participants activities such as computer training that will help them acquire the skills they need to gain employment
- Refer participants to supportive services, training and educational programs that will help make their career goals a reality

ACQUIRING JOBS TO PROMOTE HIGHER ASPIRATIONS: PROGRESS TO DATE

Since our inception last year, Claremont Neighborhood Centers, Inc. has employed a Program Coordinator/Job Developer to run Project AJPHA. Each participant attends the core program for twelve weeks and supportive services for as long as necessary. Job readiness workshops are held each week at Claremont to prepare participants for job searches, the interview process, and what to expect from the workplace environment. Topics covered in these sessions include: World of Work, Interview Do's and Don'ts, Dressing for Success, Resumes for Today, What Do Want Ads Want, and Phone Etiquette. Professionals from the community have been invited to conduct workshops, and we are networking in the community to bring in additional speakers.

In addition to offering workshops and counseling, the Program Coordinator/Job Developer recruits youth for the program, assesses their needs, and refers them to appropriate job training and supportive services at Claremont and other area youth-serving agencies. Participants are sometimes referred to our ESL Program where they receive much needed language training five nights per week. Others enter into our Adult Literacy Program where they can prepare for the GED exam and learn basic computer skills, such as typing, word processing, and spreadsheets. Our Job Developer also increases access to job opportunities by scheduling appointments for participants to utilize the City Job Bank and by working closely with local corporations.

OUTCOMES/EVALUATION

Project AJPHA's initial results have been encouraging. After the first program year, of the 31 original participants, thirteen found full-time employment, seven re-entered high school, two enrolled in community college, and six chose to attend a local business institute. Because AJPHA is a new initiative, we have had limited opportunity to track results. Currently, program staff assess job preparation, educational, and job readiness needs based on each individual's employment goals. Staff follow up with participants to track their progress in achieving these goals on a periodic basis. As described below we are seeking funding to strengthen AJPHA's evaluation component.

PLANS FOR PROGRAM ENRICHMENT

To increase Project AJPHA's effectiveness, we plan to implement program enhancements that will enable us to assist more young people, provide additional job readiness workshops and training, and offer internship positions at area corporations. The Project has grown from assisting 30 young people in its first year to our current capacity of 75. We have a waiting list of 45. With these program enhancements Claremont seeks to ensure the best chances for a hopeful future for these young people.

Job Readiness Training
Computer training courses are offered at Claremont each night. We have 17 computers in our computer lab and can serve up to 34 students at any given time. For many Project AJPHA students this is their first time using a computer. Additional funding to increase the number of hours the Computer Instructor is available to work with Project AJPHA will ensure that students receive adequate time for resume preparation, cover letter writing, and the training that they need to be competitive for entry-level jobs.

Real World Job Experience
Our Program Coordinator is negotiating with area corporations, including a major local health plan and an insurance company, to set up internship positions for Project AJPHA participants. Internships will provide the opportunity to develop real

world job experience and will help applicants acquire workplace skills. These employment opportunities will help build the interns' confidence and self-esteem as they enhance their job skills. The Program Coordinator will follow up with both the intern and the intern's supervisor to ensure a positive experience for all involved.

Follow-up and Evaluation

We recognize that the most effective job preparation programs offer participants ongoing support and counseling. Claremont is seeking to be available to Project AJPHA participants and graduates in case they encounter difficulties at work or in school. The Program Coordinator/Job Developer will follow up with program graduates to ensure that they are supported as they complete job training courses, complete their high school education, or adjust to a new work situation. The Program Coordinator/Job Developer will be available to assist those who want to change career or educational plans, or begin new job searches.

Increased follow-up will also provide a means to measure program effectiveness in greater detail. By increasing our efforts to contact former participants over a period of time, we will more effectively be able to identify best practices and areas that need improvement. We will also be able to measure key factors such as job retention, turnover, promotion, acquisition of benefits and salaries earned.

STAFFING

Rachel Spivey has been Claremont Neighborhood Centers, Inc.'s Executive Director since 1979. She is responsible for program supervision. Under her guidance, Claremont Neighborhood Centers, Inc. has become a vital force in the community, where residents know they can find the support and services they need to improve their lives.

A Program Coordinator/Job Developer who reports to the Executive Director oversees the day-to-day operations of Project AJPHA. AJPHA's Program Coordinator has extensive experience as a job developer and counselor. She brings with her an in-depth knowledge of community resources and needs. The

Program Coordinator also oversees the work of the Computer Instructor.

Our plans for program enhancement include the hiring of an additional staff person, a Job Developer Assistant, who will be responsible for participant registration and overall administrative support including help with follow-up, internship placement and evaluation. This support will allow our Program Coordinator more time to provide counseling, coordinate workshops, conduct outreach and network with area agencies and corporations.

SUSTAINABILITY

In the short time since its inception, we have seen the importance of Project AJPHA to the men and women of our community. Claremont is committed to offering Project AJPHA on an ongoing basis. Claremont has a proven record of creating programs and attracting the funding necessary to sustain operations and facilitate growth. With Project AJPHA we intend to secure a base of funding from corporations and foundations. We have begun outreach to foundations and corporations with a known interest in funding job readiness programs serving minority populations. We will maintain an ongoing systematic and consistent approach to potential funders. We also hope to receive city and state funding, which will cover a small percentage of the budget each year.

CLAREMONT NEIGHBORHOOD CENTERS, INC.

Claremont Neighborhood Centers, Inc. serves the South Bronx community of Claremont/Morrisania. For nearly four decades, The Center has served as an oasis for thousands of Claremont/Morrisania residents. Claremont is the only facility of its kind within a 20-block radius. Fifty-five percent of our residents are African American and 45% are Latinos. Of the approximately 10,000 residents of Claremont Village, over 40% are under 21 years of age.

The Claremont/Morrisania neighborhood has a high incidence of unemployment, drug abuse, HIV/AIDS infections, and criminal activity. The Center provides basic and vital social services including counseling, recreation activities, and educational enhancement for residents of all ages. Claremont provides linkages with other community agencies and provides referrals for services not available at the Center. The services offered at Claremont build self-reliance and foster personal, educational, and professional achievement. They are essential for community residents who seek to improve their own lives and the lives of their families.

CONCLUSION

Claremont Neighborhood Centers, Inc. is committed to building and strengthening the offerings of Project AJPHA. This year we are seeking to increase the quality and effectiveness of Project AJPHA while building a stable funding base. We hope that the Early Riser Fund will provide a grant of $25,000 to help us ensure the best chances for a hopeful future for the young people in the Claremont/Morrisania community.

PROGRAM BUDGET

EXPENSES
Personnel

Executive Director (15% of full-time expense)	$ 9,037
Administrative Assistant (15 hrs per week @ 10.17 per hour)	7,932
Program Coordinator/Job Developer full-time @35 hours per week)	21,000
Computer Instructor (15 hrs per week @ 15.00 per hour)	11,700
Job Developer Assistant (20 hrs week @ 9.50 per hour)	9,800
Fringe Benefits (@ 15%)	8,920
Total Personnel Expense	**$68,389**

Non-Personnel

Stipends for Intern	$ 4,400
Community Outreach Materials (brochures, flyers, etc.)	600
Job Readiness Workshop Materials (handouts, etc.)	1,400
Office Equipment	1,400
Office Supplies	1,100
Telephone	1,100
Postage	1,200
Printing	1,200
Staff Travel	1,200
Professional Development	700
Total Non-Personnel Expense	**$14,300**
Total Project AJPHA Expense	**$82,689**

Attachments

Agency Background

I.R.S. Letter of Determination

Agency Budget

Audited Financial Statement

Board of Directors

Corporate and Foundation Supporters

APPENDIX B

Selected Resources on Proposal Development

Compiled by Sarah Collins, Manager, Bibliographic Services
The Foundation Center

Barbato, Joseph and Danielle S. Furlich. *Writing for a Good Cause: The Complete Guide to Crafting Proposals and Other Persuasive Pieces for Nonprofits.* New York, NY: Simon & Schuster, 2000.
> Practical advice about the art and craft of writing related to fundraising proposals, as well as case statements, newsletters, and other communications devices used by a typical development office.

Belcher, Jane C. and Julia M. Jacobsen. *From Idea to Funded Projects: Grant Proposals That Work.* 4th revised ed. Phoenix, AZ: Oryx Press, 1992.
> Presents a method for nurturing an idea from inception through the development of a proposal; finding sources of support; administering grants; and evaluating your program.

Bowman, Joel P., and Bernardine P. Branchaw. *How to Write Proposals That Produce*. Phoenix, AZ: Oryx Press, 1992.
> A detailed and technical treatment of the process of writing proposals. Directed toward readers from both the corporate and nonprofit sectors.

Carlson, Mim. *Winning Grants Step by Step*. San Francisco, CA: Support Centers of America, 1995.
> Contains exercises designed to help with proposal planning and writing skills and to meet the requirements of both government agencies and private funders.

Friedland, Andrew J., and Carol L. Folt. *Writing Successful Science Proposals*. New Haven, CT: Yale University Press, 2000.
> Proposal writing wisdom specifically for those in scientific fields.

Hale, Phale D., Jr. *Writing Grant Proposals that Win*. 2nd ed. Washington, DC: Capitol Publications, 1997.
> Covers the major elements in any proposal and discusses the difference between applying to federal and private-sector funders.

Kosztolanyi, Istvan. *Proposal Writing*. (English ed.). Baltimore, MD: Johns Hopkins University Institute for Policy Studies, 1997.
> Outlines the standard elements of a grantseeking proposal and includes a handy checklist. Pamphlet specifically developed for nonprofit managers in Central and Eastern Europe; also available in Bulgarian, Czech, Hungarian, Polish, Russian, Slovak, and Slovene languages.

Miner, Lynn E., Jeremy T. Miner and Jerry Griffith. *Proposal Planning and Writing*. 2nd ed. Phoenix, AZ: Oryx Press, 1998.
> Covers the proposal development process for federal government, private foundation, and corporate funding sources.

Nugent, Carole and Tom Ezell. *The Grantwriter's Start-Up Kit: A Beginner's Guide to Grant Proposals* [video recording]. San Francisco, CA: Jossey-Bass Publishers, 2000.
> Discusses the key elements of grant proposals; accompanied by a workbook.

Orlich, Donald C. *Designing Successful Grant Proposals*. Alexandria, VA: Association for Supervision and Curriculum Development, 1996.
> Presents the standard elements of grant writing, with checklists.

Winning Strategies for Developing Grant Proposals. Washington, DC: Government Information Services, 1999.
> Presents general guidelines for writing proposals and specific instructions for creating proposals for private sector sources and federal agencies. Actual successful proposals are provided for each type of funder.

Zimmerman, Robert M. *Grantseeking: A Step-by-Step Approach*, rev. ed. San Francisco, CA: Zimmerman, Lehman & Associates, 1998.
> Directed to novices in the field, the book explains how to write a letter of intent, with a sample; how to create a good proposal and budget; how to follow up with funders; and the role of the board of directors in this process.

Internet resources

Elements of a Grant Proposal (www.silcom.com/~paladin/promaster.html)
> Information on proposal writing compiled by the Center for Nonprofit Management in Los Angeles, CA.

Foundation Center's Proposal Writing Short Course (www.fdncenter.org/onlib/shortcourse/prop1.html)
> Basic information about proposal writing, excerpted from *The Foundation Center's Guide to Proposal Writing*.

Non-Profit Guides (www.npguides.org/grant.htm)
Offers sample letters of inquiry as well as various proposal formats.

SERA (www.sera.com/resources/templates.html)
Includes brief instructions and templates for a letter of inquiry, proposal, cover letter proposal, and budget. Templates are available in HTML or MS Word.

APPENDIX C

Resources of the
Foundation Center

The Foundation Center is a national service organization founded and supported by foundations to provide a single authoritative source of information on foundation and corporate giving. The Center's programs are designed to help grantseekers select those funders which may be most interested in their projects from the more than 58,000 active U.S. grantmakers. Among its primary activities toward this end are publishing reference books and CD-ROMS; offering online searchable databases on foundation and corporate philanthropy; disseminating information on grantmaking, grant-seeking, and related subjects through its site on the World Wide Web; conducting a variety of educational and training programs; and operating a nationwide network of library/learning centers and Cooperating Collections.

Publications of the Foundation Center are the primary working tools of every serious grantseeker. They are also used by grantmakers, scholars, journalists, and legislators—in short, by anyone seeking any type of factual information on philanthropy. All private foundations and a significant number of corporate grantmakers actively engaged in grantmaking, regardless of size or geographic location, are included in one or more of the Center's publications. The publications are of three kinds: directories that describe specific funders, characterizing their program interests and providing fiscal and personnel data; grants indexes that list and classify by subject recent foundation and corporate awards; and guides, monographs, and bibliographies that introduce the reader to funding research, elements of proposal writing, and nonprofit management issues.

For those who wish to access information on grantmakers and their grants electronically, the Center issues *FC Search: The Foundation Center's Database on CD-ROM* containing 53,000 grantmakers and more than 210,000 associated grants. *The Foundation Directory on CD-ROM* and *The Foundation Directory Online* are searchable electronic databases that provide access to over 10,000 of the nation's largest foundations. *The Foundation Directory Online Plus* contains the top 10,000+ foundations plus a searchable database of 100,000+ grants. *The Foundation Directory Online Premium* includes 20,000+ foundations plus 100,000+ grants. In addition, the Center's award-winning Web site features a wide array of free information about the philanthropic community.

The Foundation Center's publications and electronic products may be ordered from the Foundation Center, 79 Fifth Avenue, New York, NY 10003-3076, or online at our Web site. For more information about any aspect of the Center's programs or for the name of the Center's library collection nearest you, call 1-800-424-9836, or visit us on the Web at http://www.fdncenter.org. Please visit our Web site for the most current information available on new products and services of the Foundation Center.

GENERAL RESEARCH DIRECTORIES

THE FOUNDATION DIRECTORY, 2000 Edition

The Foundation Directory includes the latest information on all foundations whose assets exceed $3 million or whose annual grants total $200,000 or more. The 2000 Edition includes over 10,000 of these foundations, over 1,700 of which are new to this edition. *Directory* foundations hold more than $358 billion in assets and award $17 billion in grants annually.

Each *Directory* entry contains precise information on application procedures, giving limitations, types of support awarded, the publications of each foundation, and foundation staff. In addition, each entry features such vital information as the grantmaker's giving interests, financial data, grant amounts, address, and telephone number. This edition includes over 35,000 selected grants. The Foundation Center works closely with foundations to ensure the accuracy and timeliness of the information provided.

The *Directory* includes indexes by foundation name; subject areas of interest; names of donors, officers, and trustees; geographic location; international interests; types of support awarded; and grantmakers new to the volume. Also included are analyses of the foundation community by geography, asset and grant size, and the different foundation types.

Also available on CD-ROM and Online.
March 2000 / ISBN 0-87954-894-0 / $215
Published annually

THE FOUNDATION DIRECTORY PART 2, 2000 Edition

Following in the tradition of *The Foundation Directory, The Foundation Directory Part 2* covers the next largest set of foundations, those with assets from $1 million and less than $3 million or grant programs from $50,000 and less than $200,000. It includes *Directory*-level information on mid-sized foundations, an important group of grantmakers responsible for millions of dollars in funding annually. Data on over 8,700 foundations is included along with more than 29,000 recently awarded foundation grants. Access to foundation entries is facilitated by seven indexes, including foundation name; subject areas of interest; names of donors, officers, and trustees; geographic location; international interests; types of support awarded; and grantmakers new to the volume.

March 2000 / ISBN 0-87954-895-9 / $185
Published annually

THE FOUNDATION DIRECTORY SUPPLEMENT

The Foundation Directory Supplement provides the latest information on *Foundation Directory* and *Foundation Directory Part 2* grantmakers six months after those volumes are published. Each year, thousands of policy and staff changes occur at these foundations. The *Supplement* ensures that users of the *Directory* and *Directory Part 2* have the latest addresses, contact names,

policy statements, application guidelines, and financial data for the founda-
tions they're approaching for funding.
September 2000 / ISBN 0-87954-896-7 / $125
Published annually

GUIDE TO U.S. FOUNDATIONS, THEIR TRUSTEES, OFFICERS, AND DONORS

This fundraising reference tool provides current, accurate information on
47,500 private grantmaking foundations in the U.S. The two-volume set also
includes a master list of the names of the people who establish, oversee, and
manage those institutions. Fundraisers can facilitate their funding research
by discovering the philanthropic connections of current donors, board
members, volunteers, and prominent families in their geographic area. Each
entry includes asset and giving amounts as well as geographic limitations.

The *Guide to U.S. Foundations* is the only source of published data on
thousands of local foundations. (It includes more than 27,000 grantmakers
not covered in other print publications.) Each entry also tells you whether
you can find more extensive information on the grantmaker in another
Foundation Center reference work.
April 2000 / 0-87954-897-5 / $215
Published annually

THE FOUNDATION 1000

The Foundation 1000 provides access to extensive and accurate information
on the 1,000 largest foundations in the country. *Foundation 1000* grantmakers
hold over $234 billion in assets and each year award close to 250,000 grants
worth $10 billion to nonprofit organizations nationwide.

The *Foundation 1000* provides the most thorough analyses available of the
1,000 largest foundations and their extensive grant programs. Each multi-
page foundation profile features a full foundation portrait, a detailed breakdown of the foundation's grant programs, and extensive lists of recently
awarded foundation grants.

Five indexes help fundraisers target potential funders in a variety of
ways: by subject field, type of support, geographic location, international
giving, and the names of foundation officers, donors, and trustees.
November 2000 / ISBN 0-87954-913-0 / $295
Published annually

NATIONAL DIRECTORY OF CORPORATE GIVING, 6th Edition

The *National Directory of Corporate Giving* features detailed portraits of close
to 1,900 company-sponsored foundations plus 1,000+ direct corporate giving programs. Fundraisers will find essential information on these corporate
grantmakers, including application information, key personnel, types of
support generally awarded, giving limitations, financial data, and purpose
and activities statements. Also included in the 6th Edition are over 6,500
selected grants. These grants give you the best indication of a grantmaker's
funding priorities by identifying nonprofits it has already funded. The

volume also provides data on the companies that have foundations and/or direct-giving programs. Each entry gives the company's name and address, a listing of its types of business, its financial data (complete with *Forbes* and *Fortune* ratings), a listing of its subsidiaries, divisions, plants, and offices, and a charitable-giving statement.

The *National Directory of Corporate Giving* also features an extensive bibliography and indexes.

October 1999 / ISBN 0-87954-888-6 / $195
Published biennially

CORPORATE FOUNDATION PROFILES, 11th Edition

This biennially updated volume includes comprehensive information on 207 of the largest corporate foundations in the U.S., grantmakers that each give at least $1.2 million annually. Each profile includes foundation giving interests, application guidelines, recently awarded grants, information on the sponsoring company, and many other essential fundraising facts. A section on financial data provides a summary of the size and grantmaking capacity of each foundation and contains a list of assets, gifts or contributions, grants paid, operating programs, expenditures, scholarships, and loans. A quick-scan appendix lists core financial data on some 1,300 additional corporate foundations, all of which give at least $50,000 in grants every year. Five indexes help grantseekers search for prospective funders by names of donors, officers, trustees, and staff; subject area; types of support; geographic region; and international giving.

March 2000 / ISBN 0-87954-867-3 / $155
Published biennially

SOUTHEASTERN FOUNDATIONS II: A Profile of the Region's Grantmaking Community, 2nd Edition

Southeastern Foundations II provides a detailed examination of foundation philanthropy in the 12-state Southeast region. The report includes an overview of the Southeast's share of all U.S. foundations, measures the growth of Southeastern foundations since 1992, profiles Southeastern funders by type, size, and geographic focus, compares broad giving trends of Southeastern and all U.S. foundations in 1992 and 1997, and details giving by non-Southeastern grantmakers to recipients in the region. Produced in cooperation with the Southeastern Council of Foundations.

November 1999 / ISBN 0-87954-775-8 / $19.95

NEW YORK STATE FOUNDATIONS: A Comprehensive Directory, 6th Edition

New York State Foundations offers fundraisers complete coverage of over 7,000 independent, corporate, and community foundations that fund New York nonprofits. Close to 5,900 of these foundations are located in New York state. An additional 1,200+ are out-of-state grantmakers with a documented interest in New York. Every entry has been drawn from the most current sources of information available, including IRS 990-PF returns and, in many cases, from the foundations themselves. The volume includes descriptions of 12,600 recently awarded grants. Six indexes offer quick access to foundations according to their fields of interest; international interests; types of support awarded; city and county; names of donors, officers, and trustees; and foundation names.

July 1999 / ISBN 0-87954-891-6 / $180
Published biennially

DIRECTORY OF MISSOURI GRANTMAKERS, 3rd Edition

The *Directory of Missouri Grantmakers* provides a comprehensive guide to grantmakers in the state—approximately 1,000 foundations, corporate giving programs, and public charities—from the largest grantmakers to local family foundations. Entries list giving amounts, fields of interest, purpose statements, selected grants, and more. Indexes help you target funders by subject interest, types of support, and names of key personnel.

July 1999 / ISBN 0-87954-884-3 / $75
Published biennially

FOUNDATION GRANTS TO INDIVIDUALS, 11th Edition

The only publication devoted entirely to foundation grant opportunities for qualified individual applicants, the 11th Edition of this volume features more than 3,800 entries, all of which profile foundation grants to individuals. Entries include foundation addresses and telephone numbers, financial data, giving limitations, and application guidelines.

Also available on CD-ROM
May 1999 / ISBN 0-87954-883-5 / $65
Published biennially

SUBJECT DIRECTORIES

The Foundation Center's National Guide to Funding series is designed to facilitate grantseeking within specific fields of nonprofit activity. Each of the directories described below performs a crucial step of fundraising research by identifying a set of grantmakers that have already stated or demonstrated an interest in a particular field. Entries provide access to foundation addresses, financial data, giving priorities, application procedures, contact names, and key officials. Many entries also feature recently awarded grants, the best indication of a grantmaker's funding priorities. A variety of indexes help fundraisers target potential grant sources by subject area, geographic preferences, types of support, and the names of donors, officers, and trustees.

Subject guides are published biennially.

GUIDE TO FUNDING FOR INTERNATIONAL AND FOREIGN PROGRAMS, 5th Edition

The *Guide to Funding for International and Foreign Programs* covers over 1,000 grantmakers interested in funding projects with an international focus, both

within the U.S. and abroad. Program areas covered include international relief, disaster assistance, human rights, civil liberties, community development, education, and more. The volume also includes descriptions of more than 8,900+ recently awarded grants.
May 2000 / ISBN 0-87954-903-3 / $125

NATIONAL GUIDE TO FUNDING IN AGING, 6th Edition

This volume provides essential facts on close to 1,400 grantmakers with a specific interest in the field of aging. This funding tool includes up-to-date addresses, financial data, giving priorities statements, application procedures, contact names, and key officials. The volume also provides recent grants lists with descriptions of over 2,200 grants for nearly 500 foundation entries. Section II of this volume includes basic descriptions and contact information for approximately 85 voluntary organizations that offer valuable technical assistance or information to older Americans and the agencies that serve them.
June 2000 / ISBN 0-87954-904-1/ $115

NATIONAL GUIDE TO FUNDING IN AIDS, 1st Edition

This volume covers more than 600 foundations, corporate giving programs, and public charities that support AIDS- and HIV-related nonprofit organizations involved in direct relief, medical research, legal aid, preventative education, and other programs aimed at empowering persons with AIDS and AIDS-related diseases. Over 760 recently awarded grants show the types of projects funded by grantmakers.
July 1999 / ISBN 0-87954-882-7 / $75

NATIONAL GUIDE TO FUNDING IN ARTS AND CULTURE, 6th Edition

This volume covers more than 7,500 grantmakers with an interest in funding art colonies, dance companies, museums, theaters, and other types of arts and culture projects and institutions. The volume also includes more than 16,500 descriptions of recently awarded grants.
May 2000 / ISBN 0-87954-906-8 / $155

NATIONAL GUIDE TO FUNDING FOR CHILDREN, YOUTH AND FAMILIES, 5th Edition

The *National Guide to Funding for Children, Youth and Families* provides access to essential facts on over 5,100 grantmakers that together award millions of dollars each year to organizations committed to causes involving children, youth, and families. Each entry includes the grantmaker's address and contact person, purpose statement, and application guidelines. Grantseekers will also find useful descriptions of over 19,100 sample grants recently awarded by many of these foundations.
June 1999 / ISBN 0-87954-877-0 / $150

NATIONAL GUIDE TO FUNDING FOR ELEMENTARY AND SECONDARY EDUCATION, 5th Edition

This volume provides information on more than 3,300 grantmakers that support nursery schools, bilingual education initiatives, remedial reading/math programs, drop-out prevention services, educational testing programs, and many other nonprofit organizations and initiatives. The volume also includes descriptions of over 8,800 recently awarded grants.

July 1999 / ISBN 0-87954-880-0 / $140

NATIONAL GUIDE TO FUNDING FOR INFORMATION TECHNOLOGY, 2nd Edition

This volume provides essential facts on over 700 grantmakers that award grants to projects involving information technology. The guide also includes descriptions of over 2,400 recently awarded grants for computer science, engineering and technology, telecommunications, and media and communications.

June 1999 / ISBN 0-87954-879-7 / $115

NATIONAL GUIDE TO FUNDING FOR THE ENVIRONMENT AND ANIMAL WELFARE, 5th Edition

This guide covers over 2,900 grantmakers that fund nonprofits involved in international conservation, ecological research, waste reduction, animal welfare, and more. The volume also includes descriptions of over 7,200 recently awarded grants.

May 2000 / ISBN 0-87954-907-6 / $115

NATIONAL GUIDE TO FUNDING IN HEALTH, 6th Edition

The *National Guide to Funding in Health* contains essential facts on over 7,700 grantmakers interested in funding hospitals, universities, research institutes, community-based agencies, national health associations, and a broad range of other health-related programs and services. The volume also includes descriptions of more than 16,900 recently awarded grants.

June 1999 / ISBN 0-87954-876-2 / $150

NATIONAL GUIDE TO FUNDING IN HIGHER EDUCATION, 6th Edition

The *National Guide to Funding in Higher Education* includes information on over 7,200 grantmakers with an interest in funding colleges, universities, graduate programs, and research institutes, as well as descriptions of more than 18,000 recently awarded grants.

June 2000 / ISBN 0-87954-905-X / $175

NATIONAL GUIDE TO FUNDING FOR LIBRARIES AND INFORMATION SERVICES, 5th Edition

This volume provides essential data on 880 grantmakers that support a wide range of organizations and initiatives, from the smallest public libraries to major research institutions, academic/research libraries, art, law, and

medical libraries, and other specialized information centers. The volume also includes descriptions of close to 1,600 recently awarded grants.
June 1999 / ISBN 0-87954-878-9 / $95

NATIONAL GUIDE TO FUNDING IN RELIGION, 5th Edition

With this volume, fundraisers who work for nonprofits affiliated with religious organizations have access to information on over 6,700 grantmakers that have demonstrated or stated an interest in funding churches, missionary societies, religious welfare and education programs, and many other types of projects and institutions. The volume also includes descriptions of more than 8,000 recently awarded grants.
May 1999 / ISBN 0-87954-875-4 / $140

NATIONAL GUIDE TO FUNDING FOR WOMEN AND GIRLS, 5th Edition

This volume covers over 1,200 grantmakers with an interest in funding such projects as rape prevention programs, shelters for abused women, girls' clubs, health clinics, employment centers, and various other programs. The volume also provides descriptions of 5,400 recently awarded grants.
July 1999 / ISBN 0-87954-881-9 / $115

GRANT DIRECTORIES

GRANT GUIDES

Designed for fundraisers who work within defined fields of nonprofit development, this series of guides lists actual foundation grants of $10,000 or more in 25 key areas of grantmaking.

Each title in the series affords access to the names, addresses, and giving limitations of the foundations listed. The grant descriptions provide fundraisers with the grant recipient's name and location; the amount of the grant; the date the grant was authorized; and a summary of the grant's intended use.

In addition, each *Grant Guide* includes three indexes: the type of organization generally funded by the grantmaker, the subject focus of the foundation's grants, and the geographic area in which the foundation has already funded projects.

Each *Grant Guide* also includes a concise overview of the foundation spending patterns within the specified field. The introduction uses a series of statistical tables to document such important findings as: (1) the 25 top funders in your area of interest (by total dollar amount of grants); (2) the 15 largest grants reported; (3) the total dollar amount and number of grants awarded for specific types of support, recipient organization type, and population group; and (4) the total grant dollars received in each U.S. state and many foreign countries.
Series published annually in December / 2000 / 2001 Editions / $75 each

THE FOUNDATION GRANTS INDEX, 2001 Edition

A foundation's recently awarded grants offer the best indication of its future funding priorities. The 2001 (29th) Edition of *The Foundation Grants Index* is the most current and accurate source of information on recent grantmaker awards. The *Grants Index* now covers the grantmaking programs of over 1,000 of the largest independent, corporate, and community foundations in the U.S. and includes more than 97,000 grant descriptions in all.

Grant descriptions are divided into 28 broad subject areas, such as health, higher education, and arts and culture. Within each of these broad fields, the grant descriptions are listed geographically by state and alphabetically by the name of the foundation, an arrangement that helps fundraisers find prospective funders that share their program interests *and* that fund projects within their geographic region.

December 2000 / ISBN 0-87954-914-9 / $165

GUIDEBOOKS, MANUALS, AND REPORTS

AIDS FUNDRAISING

Published in conjunction with Funders Concerned About AIDS, this guide helps nonprofit groups plan a strategy for raising money. *AIDS Fundraising* covers a vast array of money-generating initiatives, from membership drives to special events, direct mail, and others.

July 1991 / ISBN 0-87954-390-6 / $10

ARTS FUNDING: A Report on Foundation Trends, 3rd Edition

This report focuses on grantmaking in 1996 and analyzes over 11,000 arts grants awarded by 800+ foundations, providing a detailed picture of giving priorities in the field. This edition of *Arts Funding* includes an analysis of arts grantmakers and recipients by region, an examination of the impact of smaller grants on the field, and brief profiles of arts grantmakers that support individual artists.

November 1998 / ISBN 0-87954-813-4 / $19.95

ARTS FUNDING 2000: Funder Perspectives on Current and Future Trends

by Loren Renz and Caron Atlas

Arts Funding 2000 explores the current state of arts grantmaking and previews emerging themes and issues. Based on in-depth interviews with 35 leading foundations and corporations nationwide, conducted in 1999, the report offers an inside perspective on recent changes in arts funding priorities and strategies and on factors affecting decision-making. Important issues and opportunities facing the arts community and arts funders at the turn of the century are identified. Conducted in cooperation with Grantmakers in the Arts.

November 1999 / ISBN 0-87954-776-6 / $14.95

FAMILY FOUNDATIONS: A Profile of Funders and Trends

Family Foundations is an essential resource for anyone interested in under-standing the fastest growing segment of foundation philanthropy. The report provides the most comprehensive measurement to date of the size and scope of the U.S. family foundation community. The report identifies the number of family foundations and their distribution by region and state, size, geographic focus, and decade of establishment; and includes analyses of staffing and public reporting by these funders. *Family Foundations* also examines trends in giving by a sample of larger family foundations between 1993 and 1998 and compares these patterns with independent foundations overall. Prepared in cooperation with the National Center for Family Philanthropy.
August 2000 / ISBN 0-87954-917-3 / $19.95

HEALTH POLICY GRANTMAKING: A Report on Foundation Trends

Health Policy Grantmaking explores broad trends in grantmaker support for health policy-related activities during the 1990s, a period of dramatic growth in health policy funding. This report investigates health policy's share of all giving for health, presents areas of growth in health policy fund-ing, spotlights emerging topics in the field, and identifies leading grant-makers by amount of funding and programmatic interests.
September 1998 / ISBN 0-87954-814 -2 / $14.95

INTERNATIONAL GRANTMAKING II:
An Update on U.S. Foundation Trends, 2nd Edition

An update to 1997's groundbreaking *International Grantmaking* study, this report documents trends in international giving by U.S. foundations in the late 1990s. Based on a sample of over 570 foundations, *International Grantmaking II* identifies shifts in international giving priorities, types of support provided, recipients funded, and countries/regions targeted for support. The report also includes an overview of recent events and factors shaping the international funding environment; and perspectives on the changing funding climate based on a 2000 survey of more than 25 leading international grantmakers. Prepared in cooperation with the Council on Foundations.
November 2000 / ISBN 0-87954-916-5 / $35

THE FOUNDATION CENTER'S GRANTS CLASSIFICATION SYSTEM INDEXING MANUAL WITH THESAURUS, Revised Edition

A "how-to" guide, the *Grants Classification Manual* includes a complete set of all classification codes to facilitate precise tracking of grants and recipients by subject, recipient type, and population categories. It also features a com-pletely revised thesaurus to help identify the "official" terms and codes that represent thousands of subject areas and recipient types in the Center's sys-tem of grants classification.
May 1995 / ISBN 0-87954-644-1 / $95

FOUNDATION FUNDAMENTALS: A Guide for Grantseekers, 6th Edition

This comprehensive, easy-to-read guidebook shows you how to use print and electronic funding research directories and databases to develop your prospect list; how to use the World Wide Web to locate information on potential funders; how to target grantmakers by subject interest, types of support, and geographic area; how to shape your proposal to reflect the special concerns of corporate funders; and more. The 6th Edition is fully revised with up-to-date charts and worksheets.
August 1999 / ISBN 0-87954-869-X / $24.95

THE FOUNDATION CENTER'S USER-FRIENDLY GUIDE: A Grantseeker's Guide to Resources, 4th Edition

This book answers the most commonly asked questions about grantseeking in an upbeat, easy-to-read style. Specifically designed for novice grantseekers, the *User-Friendly Guide* leads the reader through the maze of unfamiliar jargon and wide range of research guides used successfully by professional fundraisers every day.
July 1996 / ISBN 0-87954-666-2 / $14.95

FOUNDATIONS TODAY SERIES, 2000 Edition

The successor to the Foundation Center's popular *Foundation Giving* report, the *Foundations Today Series* provides the latest information on foundation growth and trends in foundation giving. A subscription to the 2000 Edition of the *Foundations Today Series* includes copies of all four reports and the estimates update (as they are published).

Foundation Giving Trends: Update on Funding Priorities—Examines 1998 grantmaking patterns of a sample of more than 1,000 larger U.S. foundations and compares current giving priorities with trends since 1980. *January 2000*

Foundation Growth and Giving Estimates: 1999 Preview—Provides a first look at estimates of foundation giving for 1999 and final statistics on actual giving and assets for 1998. Presents new top 100 foundation lists. *March 2000*

Foundation Yearbook: Facts and Figures on Private and Community Foundations—Documents the growth in number, giving, and assets of all active U.S. foundations from 1975 through 1998. *June 2000*

Foundation Staffing: Update on Staffing Trends of Private and Community Foundations—Examines changes in the staffing patterns of U.S. foundations through mid-2000, based on an annual survey of nearly 3,000 staffed foundations. *September 2000*

Foundation Reporting: Update on Public Reporting Trends of Private and Community Foundations—Documents changes in voluntary reporting patterns of U.S. foundations through mid-2000, based on an annual survey of more than 3,000 foundations that issued publications. *November 2000*
Annual 2000 / ISBN 0-87954-898-3 / $95

THE FOUNDATION CENTER'S GUIDE TO GRANTSEEKING ON THE WEB, 2000 Edition

The *Guide to Grantseeking on the Web* provides both novice and experienced Web users with a gateway to the numerous online resources available to grantseekers. Foundation Center staff experts have team-authored this guide, contributing their extensive knowledge of Web content as well as their tips and strategies on how to evaluate and use Web-based funding materials. Presented in a concise, "how-to" style, the *Guide* will introduce you to the World Wide Web and help structure your funding research with a toolkit of resources. These resources include foundation and corporate Web sites, searchable databases for grantseeking, online government funding sources, online journals, and interactive services on the Web for grantseekers.

February 2000 / Book / ISBN 0-87954-865-7 / $19.95
CD-ROM / ISBN 0-87954-909-2 / $19.95
Book and CD-ROM / $29.95

THE PRI DIRECTORY: Charitable Loans and Other Program-Related Investments by Foundations

Some foundations have developed an alternative financing approach—known as program-related investing—for supplying capital to the non-profit sector. PRIs have been used to support community revitalization, low-income housing, microenterprise development, historic preservation, human services, and more. This directory lists leading PRI providers and includes tips on how to seek out and manage PRIs. Foundation listings include funder name and state; recipient name, city, and state (or country); and a description of the project funded. There are several helpful indexes to guide PRI-seekers to records by foundation/recipient location, subject/type of support, and recipient name, as well as an index to officers, donors, and trustees.

February 2001 / ISBN 0-87954-915-7 / $75

OTHER PUBLICATIONS

AMERICA'S NONPROFIT SECTOR: A Primer, 2nd Edition

by Lester M. Salamon

In this revised edition of his classic book, Lester M. Salamon clarifies the basic structure and role of the nonprofit sector in the U.S. Moreover, he places the nonprofit sector into context in relation to the government and business sectors. He also shows how the position of the nonprofit sector has changed over time, both generally and in the major fields in which the sector is active. Illustrated with numerous charts and tables, Salamon's book is an easy-to-understand primer for government officials, journalists, and students—in short, for anyone who wants to comprehend the makeup of America's nonprofit sector.

February 1999 / ISBN 0-87954-801-0 / $14.95

BEST PRACTICES OF EFFECTIVE NONPROFIT ORGANIZATIONS: A Practitioner's Guide

by Philip Bernstein

Philip Bernstein has drawn on his own extensive experience as a nonprofit executive, consultant, and volunteer to produce this review of "best practices" adopted by successful nonprofit organizations. The author identifies and explains the procedures which provide the foundation for social achievement in all nonprofit fields. Topics include defining purposes and goals, creating comprehensive financing plans, evaluating services, and effective communication.

February 1997 / ISBN 0-87954-755-3 / $29.95

THE BOARD MEMBER'S BOOK, 2nd Edition

by Brian O'Connell

Based on his extensive experience working with and on the boards of voluntary organizations, Brian O'Connell has developed this practical guide to the essential functions of voluntary boards. O'Connell offers practical advice on how to be a more effective board member as well as on how board members can help their organizations make a difference. He also provides an extensive reading list.

October 1993 / ISBN 0-87954-502-X / $24.95

CAREERS FOR DREAMERS AND DOERS: A Guide to Management Careers in the Nonprofit Sector

by Lilly Cohen and Dennis R.Young

A comprehensive guide to management positions in the nonprofit world, *Careers for Dreamers and Doers* offers practical advice for starting a job search and suggests strategies used by successful managers throughout the voluntary sector.

November 1989 / ISBN 0-87954-294-2 / $24.95

ECONOMICS FOR NONPROFIT MANAGERS

by Dennis R. Young and Richard Steinberg

Economics for Nonprofit Managers is a complete course in the economic issues faced by America's nonprofit decision-makers. Young and Steinberg introduce and explain concepts such as opportunity cost, analysis at the margin, market equilibrium, market failure, and cost-benefit analysis. This volume also focuses on issues of particular concern to nonprofits, such as the economics of fundraising and volunteer recruiting, the regulatory environment, the impact of competition on nonprofit performance, interactions among sources of revenue, and more.

July 1995 / ISBN 0-87954-610-7 / $34.95

HANDBOOK ON PRIVATE FOUNDATIONS
by David F. Freeman and the Council on Foundations

This publication provides a thorough look at the issues facing the staff and boards of private foundations in the U.S. Author David F. Freeman offers sound advice on establishing, staffing, and governing foundations and provides insights into legal and tax guidelines as well. Each chapter concludes with a useful annotated bibliography. Sponsored by the Council on Foundations.

September 1991
Softbound: ISBN 0-87954-404-X / $29.95
Hardbound: ISBN 0-87954-403-1 / $39.95

THE NONPROFIT ENTREPRENEUR: *Creating Ventures to Earn Income*
Edited by Edward Skloot

In a topic-by-topic approach to nonprofit venturing, consultant and entrepreneur Edward Skloot demonstrates how nonprofits can launch successful earned-income enterprises without compromising their missions. Skloot has compiled a collection of writings by the nation's top practitioners and advisors in nonprofit enterprise. Topics covered include legal issues, marketing techniques, business planning, avoiding the pitfalls of venturing for smaller nonprofits, and a special section on museums and their retail operations.

September 1988 / ISBN 0-87954-239-X / $19.95

A NONPROFIT ORGANIZATION OPERATING MANUAL: *Planning for Survival and Growth*
by Arnold J. Olenick and Philip R. Olenick

This straightforward, all-inclusive desk manual for nonprofit executives covers all aspects of starting and managing a nonprofit. The authors discuss legal problems, obtaining tax exemption, organizational planning and development, and board relations; operational, proposal, cash, and capital budgeting; marketing, grant proposals, fundraising, and for-profit ventures; computerization; and tax planning and compliance.

July 1991 / ISBN 0-87954-293-4 / $29.95

PEOPLE POWER: SERVICE, ADVOCACY, EMPOWERMENT
by Brian O'Connell

People Power, a selection of Brian O'Connell's most powerful writings, provides thought-provoking commentary on the nonprofit world. The 25+ essays included in this volume range from keen analyses of the role of voluntarism in American life, to sound advice for nonprofit managers, to suggestions for developing and strengthening the nonprofit sector of the future.

October 1994 / ISBN 0-87954-563-1 / $24.95

PROMOTING ISSUES AND IDEAS: A Guide to Public Relations for Nonprofit Organizations, Revised Edition

by M Booth & Associates

M Booth & Associates are specialists in promoting the issues and ideas of nonprofit groups. Their book includes the "nuts-and-bolts" of advertising, publicity, speech-making, lobbying, and special events; how to write and produce informational literature; public relations on a shoe-string budget; how to plan and evaluate PR efforts; the use of rapidly evolving communication technologies; and a new chapter on crisis management.

December 1995 / ISBN 0-87954-594-1 / $29.95

RAISE MORE MONEY FOR YOUR NONPROFIT ORGANIZATION: A Guide to Evaluating and Improving Your Fundraising

by Anne L. New

In *Raise More Money*, Anne New sets guidelines for a fundraising program that will benefit the incipient as well as the established nonprofit organization. The author divides her text into three sections: "The Basics," which delineates the necessary steps a nonprofit must take before launching a development campaign; "Fundraising Methods," which encourages organizational self-analysis and points the way to an effective program involving many sources of funding; and "Fundraising Resources," a 20-page bibliography that highlights the most useful research and funding directories available.

January 1991 / ISBN 0-87954-388-4 / $14.95

SECURING YOUR ORGANIZATION'S FUTURE: A Complete Guide to Fundraising Strategies, Revised Edition

by Michael Seltzer

This volume is recommended for novice grantseekers, experienced fundraisers, and those enrolled in nonprofit management courses. Its intent is to help organizations strengthen their capacity to successfully raise funds, diversify their revenue streams, and create long-term sustainability. Michael Seltzer supplements his text with numerous worksheets, case studies, and an extensive annotated bibliography.

February 2001 / ISBN 0-87954-900-9 / $34.95

SUCCEEDING WITH CONSULTANTS: Self-Assessment for the Changing Nonprofit

by Barbara Kibbe and Fred Setterberg

Written by Barbara Kibbe and Fred Setterberg and supported by the David and Lucile Packard Foundation, this book guides nonprofits through the process of selecting and utilizing consultants to strengthen their organization's operations. The book emphasizes self assessment tools and covers six different areas in which a nonprofit organization might benefit from a

consultant's advice: governance, planning, fund development, financial management, public relations and marketing, and quality assurance.
April 1992 / ISBN 0-87954-450-3 / $19.95

THE 21ST CENTURY NONPROFIT

by Paul B. Firstenberg

In *The 21st Century Nonprofit,* Paul B. Firstenberg encourages managers to adopt strategies developed by the for-profit sector in recent years. These strategies will help them to expand their revenue base by diversifying grant sources, exploit the possibilities of for-profit enterprises, develop human resources by learning how to attract and retain talented people, and explore the nature of leadership through short profiles of three nonprofit CEOs.
July 1996 / ISBN 0-87954-672-7 / $34.95

MEMBERSHIP PROGRAM

ASSOCIATES PROGRAM
Direct Line to Fundraising Information

The Associates Program's e-mail and toll-free telephone reference service helps you to:

- identify potential sources of foundation funding for your organization; and
- gather important information to use in targeting and presenting your proposals effectively.

Membership in the Associates Program entitles you to funding information from: foundation and corporate Web sites, annual reports, brochures, press releases, grants lists, and other announcements; IRS 990-PF information returns for all active grantmaking U.S. foundations—often the only source of information on small foundations; and books and periodicals on the grantmaking field, including regulation and nonprofit management.

- The annual fee of $595 for the Associates Program entitles you to ten free reference requests per month. Additional reference requests can be made at the rate of $30 per ten questions.
- Membership in the Associates Program allows you to request custom searches of the Foundation Center's computerized databases. There is an additional cost for this service.
- Associates Program members may request photocopies of key documents. Important information from 990-PFs, annual reports, application guidelines, and other resources can be copied and either mailed or faxed to your office. The fee for this service, available only to Associate Members, is $2.00 for the first page of material and $1.00 for each additional page. Fax service is available at an additional charge.

- All Associates Program members receive a quarterly newsletter, which provides news and information about new foundations, changes in boards of directors, new programs, and publications from the Foundation Center and other publishers in the field.

- Members are entitled to receive two special e-mail reports each month; one presenting a minimum of 75 new or emerging foundations not yet listed in our directories or on our Web site, and a second e-mail report listing current updates on grantmaker profiles.

- Associates receive an invitation to an annual conference featuring experts on trends in fundraising and philanthropy.

- Associates Program Online is a special Web site exclusively for Associates, offering online ordering, premiums and discounts, and the latest news for fundraisers.

For more information call 1-800-424-9836, or visit our World Wide Web site at http://www.fdncenter.org.

CD-ROMs

FC SEARCH: The Foundation Center's Database on CD-ROM, Version 4.0

The Foundation Center's comprehensive database of grantmakers and their associated grants can be accessed in this fully searchable CD-ROM format. *FC Search* contains the Center's entire universe of nearly 53,000 grantmaker records, including all known active foundations and corporate giving programs in the United States. It also includes over 210,000 newly reported grants from the largest foundations and the names of more than 200,000 trustees, officers, and donors which can be quickly linked to their foundation affiliations. Users can also link from *FC Search* to the Web sites of over 1,000 grantmakers and 500+ corporations.**

Grantseekers and other researchers may select multiple criteria and create customized prospect lists, which can be printed or saved. Basic or Advanced search modes and special search options enable users to make searches as broad or as specific as required. Up to 21 different criteria may be selected.

FC Search has been developed with both the novice and experienced researcher in mind. Assistance is available through Online Help, a *User Manual* that accompanies *FC Search*, as well as through a free User Hotline.

FC Search, Version 4.0, spring 2000 (prices include fall 2000 Update disk plus one User Manual).
Standalone (single user) version: $1,195
Local Area Network (2–8 users in one building) version: $1,895*
Additional copies of User Manual: $19.95
New editions of FC Search are released each spring.
Larger local area network versions, site licenses, and wide area network versions are also available.

THE FOUNDATION DIRECTORY ON CD-ROM

The Foundation Directory on CD-ROM includes over 3,800 foundation records, each of which lists approximately 10 sample grants; features a searchable index of 62,000 trustees, officers, and donors; links to over 700 foundation Web sites and the Foundation Center's Web site; includes extensive Help file and printed user guide; features Boolean operators between fields; the ability to store search schemes and mark records for use in future sessions; a wide range of printing and saving options; alphabetical or total giving sort; and the ability to affix searchable notes to personalize grantmaker records. It allows users to create customized prospect lists by selecting from 12 search fields.

The Foundation Directory on CD-ROM (includes March 2000 release and fall 2000 Update disk)
Standalone (single-user) version: $295
Local Area Network version (2–8 users in one building): $595
Larger local area network versions, site licenses, and wide area network versions are also available.

FOUNDATION GRANTS TO INDIVIDUALS ON CD-ROM

Foundation Grants to Individuals on CD-ROM includes over 4,000 foundations and public charities that provide support to individual grantseekers for research, education, general welfare, arts and culture, and more. Grantmaker records include current information: address, contact name, financial data, application information, program descriptions, and more.

The CD-ROM includes nine search fields: geographic focus, fields of interest, types of support, company name, school name, grantmaker name, grantmaker city, grantmaker state, and text search. Special features include flexible printing and saving options; the ability to mark records and save search schemes; and a searchable notepad function for devising a tickler system. In addition, the CD-ROM connects users to a special Web page with further resources for individual grantseekers.

September 2000 / Single-user / ISBN 0-87954-918-1 / $75

GUIDE TO GREATER WASHINGTON D.C. GRANTMAKERS ON CD-ROM

Compiled with the assistance of the Washington Regional Association of Grantmakers, this CD-ROM covers over 1,500 grantmakers located in the D.C. region or that have an interest in D.C.-area nonprofits. It also contains close to 1,800 selected grants and a searchable index of 8,000+ trustees, officers, and donors and their grantmaker affiliations.

Users can generate prospect lists using twelve search fields. Grantmaker portraits feature: address, phone number, contact name, financial data, giving limitations, and names of key officials. For the large foundations—those that give at least $50,000 in grants per year—the volume provides even more data, including application procedures and giving interest statements.

221

The CD-ROM links to more than 150 grantmaker Web sites; connects to a special Web page with resources of value to D.C. grantseekers; and offers flexible printing and saving options and the ability to mark records.
June 2000 / Single-user: 0-87954-912-2 / $75
Local Area Network: 0-87954-899-1 / $125

SYSTEM CONFIGURATIONS FOR CD-ROM PRODUCTS

- Windows-based PC
- Microsoft Windows™ ME, Windows™ 98, Windows™ 95, Windows™ 2000 or Windows™ NT
- Pentium microprocessor
- 16MB memory

**Internet access and Netscape's Navigator or Communicator or Microsoft's Internet Explorer browser required to access grantmaker Web sites and Foundation Center Web site.

ONLINE DATABASES

THE FOUNDATION DIRECTORY ONLINE SUBSCRIPTION SERVICE

The Foundation Directory Online

Search for prospects from among the nation's largest 10,000+ foundations. Perform searches using up to seven search fields and print results that appear in the browser window.
Monthly subscriptions start at $19.95 per month.

The Foundation Directory Online Plus

Plus service allows users to search the 10,000+ largest foundations in the U.S.—plus 100,000 grants awarded by the largest 1,000 foundations.
Monthly subscriptions start at $29.95 per month.

The Foundation Directory Online Premium

In addition to featuring 20,000 of the nation's large and mid-sized foundations—twice the number of foundations included in the other subscription services—*Premium* service includes a searchable database of 100,000 grants awarded by the top 1,000 U.S. foundations.
Monthly subscriptions start at $59.95 per month.
Foundations and grants data will be updated quarterly for the above databases. Monthly, annual, and multi-user subscription options are availabe.
Please visit www.fconline.fdncenter.org to subscribe.

DIALOG

The Center's grantmaker and grants databases are also available online through The Dialog Corporation. For further information, contact The Dialog Corporation at 1-800-334-2564.

DIALOG User Manual and Thesaurus, Revised Edition

The *User Manual and Thesaurus* is a comprehensive guide that will help you retrieve essential fundraising facts quickly and easily. It will facilitate your foundation and corporate giving research through our databases, offered online through Dialog.
November 1995 / ISBN 0-87954-595-X / $50

FOUNDATION CENTER'S WORLD WIDE WEB SITE (http://www.fdncenter.org)

Your gateway to philanthropy on the Web

The Foundation Center's World Wide Web site is fast becoming the premier online source of fundraising information. Updated and expanded on a daily basis, the Center's site provides grantseekers, grantmakers, researchers, journalists, and the general public with easy access to a range of valuable resources, among them:

- A Finding Funders directory with links to more than 1,600 individual grantmaker Web sites. The *RFP Bulletin* includes listings by subject area of requests for proposals. The bulletin is updated weekly and available via e-mail.

- Foundation Finder, a free look-up tool that provides a foundation's contact information and brief background data, such as type of foundation, assets, total giving, EIN, Web site, and link to most recent 990-PF.

- Grantmaker Web Search, a search engine that crawls the Web sites of more than 1,600 private, corporate, and community foundations, and provides relevant, accurate search results.

- 990-PF Search, a tool that searches for and downloads tax returns of private foundations. There is also a prospect worksheet to help organize your research.

- *Philanthropy News Digest,* a weekly compendium of philanthropy-related articles abstracted from major print and online media outlets. *PND* is also available via e-mail.

- A Learning Lab with comprehensive answers to FAQs, an online librarian to field questions about grantseeking and resources, and online tutorials on the grantseeking process.

- Our Proposal Writing Short Course, an extensive glossary, bibliographies, and common grant application forms.

- Information about Center-sponsored orientations, training programs, and seminars.

- The locations of more than 200 Cooperating Collections nationwide, and details on the activities and resources at our five main libraries.

- Researching Philanthropy, an online directory including *FC Stats,* free online access to more than 500 statistical tables on foundations and their giving; funding trends reports that provide the latest data available on every aspect of U.S. foundation philanthropy; and annotated links to useful resources in the nonprofit and philanthropic sectors.
- *The Literature of the Nonprofit Sector Online,* a searchable bibliographic database with nearly 19,000 entries of works in the field of philanthropy, over 11,000 of which are abstracted.
- A special section called "For Grantmakers" offers funders the opportunity to help get the word out about their work, answers frequently asked questions, and informs grantmakers on recent developments in the field and how the Center assists grantees and applicants.

The Center's publications and electronic resources can be ordered via the site's automated Marketplace. Visit our Web site often for information on new products and services.

About the Author

Jane C. Geever is chairman of the development consulting firm, J. C. Geever, Inc. The firm, founded by Ms. Geever in 1975, was the first woman-led fund raising company admitted into membership in the American Association of Fund Raising Counsel (AAFRC).

Among her achievements, she assisted in the creation of the certificate program in fund raising at New York University, spearheaded the first jobs bank at the National Society of Fund Raising Executives' (NSFRE)[*] International Conference and New York NSFRE's Fundraising Day, and was appointed to the Independent Sector's ad hoc committee on Values and Ethics. Ms. Geever is a member of the advisory council for the national project *Funding Fundraising* at Baruch College and is active in Independent Sector's *Give Five* program in New York. She has been a member of the board and officer of the NSFRE Institute and of the AAFRC.

---

[*] Now known as the Association of Fundraising Professionals.

Ms. Geever holds a Master's Degree from the New School for Social Research, and she has done post-graduate study in business management at Stanford University. She delivered the May 1989 commencement address at the 71st commencement of her alma mater, Seton Hill College in Greensburg, Pennsylvania, at which time she received an honorary Doctor of Humane Letters degree.

Ms. Geever is a nationally recognized author and lecturer. She teaches seminars in association with the Foundation Center on proposal writing and approaching foundations and corporate funders.